T0276253

AMOS OZ

Amos Oz

Writer, Activist, Icon

ROBERT ALTER

Yale

UNIVERSITY

PRESS

New Haven and London

Yale University Press books may be purchased in quantity for educational,
business, or promotional use. For information, please e-mail sales.press@yale.edu
(U.S. office) or sales@yaleup.co.uk (U.K. office).

Set in Janson Oldstyle type by Integrated Publishing Solutions.
Printed in the United States of America.

Library of Congress Control Number: 2022951526
ISBN 978-0-300-25017-6 (hardcover : alk. paper)

A catalogue record for this book is available from the British Library.

This paper meets the requirements of ANSI/NISO Z39.48-1992
(Permanence of Paper).

10 9 8 7 6 5 4 3 2 1

Frontispiece: Amos Oz, with the constant cigarette of his early career,
writing at his desk. Photo courtesy of Nily Oz.

Rogue's Progress: Studies in the Picaresque Novel
Fielding and the Nature of the Novel
After the Tradition
Partial Magic: The Novel as a Self-Conscious Genre
Defenses of the Imagination
A Lion for Love: A Critical Biography of Stendhal
The Art of Biblical Narrative
Motives for Fiction
The Art of Biblical Poetry
The Invention of Hebrew Prose: Modern Fiction
and the Language of Realism
The Pleasures of Reading in an Ideological Age
Necessary Angels: Tradition and Modernity
in Kafka, Benjamin, and Scholem
The World of Biblical Literature
Hebrew and Modernity
Canon and Creativity
Imagined Cities: Urban Experience
and the Language of the Novel
Pen of Iron: American Prose and the King James Bible
The Hebrew Bible: A Translation with Commentary
The Art of Bible Translation
Nabokov and the Real World

For Carol,
who would have been eager to read this,
in ever loving memory

CONTENTS

ACKNOWLEDGMENTS

NILY OZ provided an abundance of useful biographical information. Through my friendship with Amos, she and I have had a cordial relationship over the years. The idea for the biography—which was mine, not hers—emerged in a phone conversation we had a few months after Amos's death. I explained that this could not be an "authorized" biography, that I could be under no obligation to show any of the work in progress either to her or to her daughter Fania, and she promptly and graciously agreed. Given our personal connection, I felt constrained to exercise a certain discretion at just a couple of points in the writing, though I have been candid enough about Amos's life that one or two limited suggestions or judgments might be a little discomfiting for the Oz family. Late in the writing process, Fania was kind enough to provide several important pieces of information that enabled me to fill in a few gaps in the narrative.

The manuscript was read by Steve Zipperstein and Anita

Shapira, the co-editors of the Yale Jewish Lives series, and I thank them for their apt suggestions, most of which I have incorporated in my final version. The other reader of the manuscript was my dear friend Nitza Ben-Dov, who knew Amos well and has also been one of his most astute critics. She pointed out a few sources to which I should refer and gave me much-appreciated encouragement for what I had written.

NOTE TO THE READER

Some biographers, in an affectation of familiarity, use the subject's first name only. In my case, because he and I were friends for half a century, it would have been unnatural to do otherwise: I invariably addressed him as Amos, and he called me, since we were speaking Hebrew, by my Hebrew name, Uri. At a few points here, I use both first and last name when a public perspective on him seemed to be involved. When the family name is called for in the writer's childhood years, he is Amos Klausner, because that was before he changed his last name. In any case, I don't want readers, even reading silently, to distort the Hebrew pronunciation of his name. He should not be linked with *Amos 'n' Andy* or *The Wizard of Oz*. The first name is pronounced "AHmos," and the "o" in both names is a long vowel that rhymes with "rose" and "pose."

There are no footnotes in this biography for a simple reason: the sources for many of the details are oral communications from his widow, Nily Oz, who has been very generous in her help, and from a few others who knew him, as well as from my own interactions with him. Moreover, the published biographical sources are all in Hebrew, so references to them would not have been of much use to English readers. Almost all of Amos Oz's books have appeared in English, and his chief translator, Nicholas De Lange, has done a truly admirable job. Nevertheless, I have provided my own translations for all of the passages cited from his books because it was important for the analyses to offer a close representation of the Hebrew syntax and word choice. Professional translators, understandably, often allow themselves latitude in order to produce an aptly fluent translated text. Certain of the published translations, such as the English version of *A Tale of Love and Darkness*, reflect some abridgment, and for the purpose of a biography, I needed invariably to refer to the complete original text. Finally, there is a large body of criticism, in Hebrew and in other languages, on the novels and stories of Amos Oz, but it is predominantly literary, not biographical, exploring his style, themes, narrative structures, recurrent motifs, and so forth, so it has not been relevant to writing about his life.

AMOS OZ

1

———◆◦◆◦◆———

Childhood

READERS OF *A Tale of Love and Darkness*, numbering in the millions across the globe, perusing it in some forty-five languages, may wonder what more can be said about Amos Oz's childhood that has not already been vividly reported in this, his finest book. *A Tale*, after all, gives us an unforgettable picture of the one-bedroom basement apartment in the Jerusalem neighborhood of Kerem Avraham where he grew up in the 1940s and of the neighborhood itself and its mixed population (now it is mostly ultra-Orthodox): immigrants from different European regions, many of them thorough secularists, with a sprinkling of religious Jews, revolutionaries, anarchists, ardently militant Zionist nationalists, flocks of aspiring writers of different stripes, strident intellectual debaters, quixotic adherents of one impossible dream or another. The book also conveys the look and feel of the streets where the young Amos Klausner played and roamed: the ramshackle apartments, the stone-strewn yards, the general sense of crowding together under impoverished conditions that in some cases bordered on subsistence existence. We also learn a good deal about the young Amos's schooling, initially in a small private class, which by the age of ten brought him under the wing of the pious Zelda Schneurson, scion of a famous Hasidic line, an altogether unconventional teacher who was later widely recognized as one of the most original Hebrew poets of her time.

Most crucially, the book draws detailed portraits of Amos Klausner's mother and father, Fania Mussman Klausner and Yehuda Arieh Klausner. His father was born in 1910 in Odessa, then a vibrant and highly variegated center of Jewish life in which Hebrew and Yiddish literature flourished. It is now in Ukraine but was then part of the Russian empire. The language of the home he grew up in was Hebrew. At the age of eleven, he moved to Vilna with his parents, fleeing the Bolsheviks, who had invaded Ukraine, and enrolled in the Hebrew *gymnasium* there and then in the University of Vilna (the family origins were in Lithuania). In 1933, aspiring to an academic career, he emigrated to Palestine. Though possessing only his bachelor's degree, he was widely read in Hebrew literature and competent in sixteen or more ancient and modern languages. Yehuda met Fania, Amos's mother, in the later 1930s when both were students at the Hebrew University. A beautiful young woman two years his junior, she had grown up in Rovno, then in Poland, now in Ukraine, and had been educated in a Hebrew-language high school, one of a network of Tarbut schools—the Hebrew name means "culture"—where instruction in all subjects was conducted in Hebrew. Tarbut schools were established in eastern European countries outside the Soviet Union between the two world wars. The home she was raised in was a grand structure— her father was an affluent miller. In 1936 the business collapsed, compelling her to leave the University of Prague, where she had begun her studies, and to emigrate to Palestine. Because of the grounding she had received in the Hebrew *gymnasium*, she arrived in Palestine with an excellent preparation in the language. In all other ways, she was quite unprepared for the rude and unfamiliar new environment.

Fania and Arieh were a mismatch (she called him Arieh, not Yehuda). He was bookish, relentlessly pedantic, a constant talker seeking to cover his social awkwardness with words, repeatedly delivering himself of bad witticisms as part of his nervousness, peering out at the world through round-rimmed spectacles that converted what might have been good looks into a geekish demeanor. She, a reader of romantic and melancholy poetry and fiction in half a dozen languages, was literary in a different way. Given to protracted, often brooding silences, commanding attention when she did speak, she was sensitive to others, charming them with her grace and beauty, but as time went on, she suffered from a chronic depression that finally slid into psychosis. We shall have occasion to consider what might have attracted two such different people to each other.

The first question that should be asked about Amos Oz's account of his early years in *A Tale of Love and Darkness* is what sort of book it constitutes. He himself vacillated in the many talks and interviews he gave about it in Israel and in a wide range of countries abroad. He did not consider it to be a novel, he said, because, after all, the tale he told was anchored in his actual experience and the experience of his family, both in Palestine-Israel and in the previous generations in Europe. Yet in at least one television interview, with a young South Korean woman, he referred to it several times as a novel, and that is also the designation favored by one of his most perceptive Israeli critics, Nitza Ben-Dov. What we can say is that he deployed novelistic means in shaping the basically factual narrative of his childhood and his family. These included, as he himself noted in one of his talks on the book, inventing dialogue in instances where he could not have been present, as in his depiction of the relationship between his two eccentric Klausner grandparents,

3

who lived in Jerusalem. A novelist, moreover, is always obliged to exercise selectivity in laying out the story of his characters, and this is also true in *A Tale of Love and Darkness*. I shall address at least a couple of the aspects of his family story that he decided not to include. A novelistic shaping of a narrative is never merely a catalogue of its successive details—it is not just one damned thing after another, as E. M. Forster once said—but rather involves stamping all the details with an imaginative coherence through the style in which they are presented, the imagery through which they are seen, the links articulated between one element of the narrative and another. Such a presentation is manifestly evident in *A Tale of Love and Darkness*.

A further question pertinent to his biography is why he decided to write this book at this moment in his life. As we shall see, for almost five decades he had remained altogether silent about his mother's psychosis and especially about her suicide, which is memorably and painfully evoked in the concluding pages of *A Tale*. There is, however, one fleeting exception to this silence. In 1975, in a short piece, "A Note on Myself," reprinted three years later in the collection *In the Strong Blue Light*, he permitted himself these two quick sentences: "But Fania, my mother, could not bear her life and committed suicide in 1952 out of all her frustration or longing. Nothing had worked out." These scant words, which flash by stroboscopically, written four years before he finally spoke about his mother's end with his wife, Nily, suggest that he was struggling to come out with the dire fact but immediately pulled back because it was so painful. Perhaps he permitted himself these few words of revelation because this brief sketch of his life was written to be included in a biographical encyclopedia of writers published in New York, a venue no one in Israel was likely to notice. Only when he entered his sixties did he take the drastic step of facing head-on the trauma that continued to haunt him. I will consider in a later chapter what might have impelled him to make such a pivotal turn at that point in his life.

But what is the essential subject of *A Tale*? In one of his talks, Amos said it was really the story of his family. That is by and large true, but, as I shall propose, a different purpose needs to be added to the family story. As many readers, especially in Israel, realized at the time of its initial publication in 2002, the explosive revelation of the book was its direct account—imagined in riveting novelistic terms—of the suicide of Amos's mother when he was twelve and a half years old. Although this terrible event had been widely known to Israeli readers, who recognized that several of the plots of his stories and novels were transpositions in fictional terms of his mother's suicide, Amos could not bring himself to speak about it for many years. It is almost shocking to learn that he did not breathe a word of it to his wife until 1979, nineteen years after the beginning of what was a marriage of intimate sharing. The first time he addressed the suicide in some detail, though rather intermittently, in any of his books was in *The Same Sea*, an experimental novel in verse with certain autobiographical elements that came out just three years before *A Tale of Love and Darkness*. At this stage of his life, then, as he turned sixty, he was moving toward a full confrontation in writing with the traumatizing act that had deeply troubled him through the years. But this confrontation was not really cathartic for him. As we shall see, at the end of his life he still felt the sharp pain of the psychological wound inflicted on him by what he felt was his mother's abrupt abandonment of him.

It is a mistake, however, to think that the mother's suicide is the "real" subject of the book. A signal instance of this mistake is in an article by the talented Hebrew novelist Rubi Namdar in a 2020 issue of the *Jewish Review of Books*. Namdar is an intelligent and literarily sensitive writer, but I think he slipped into a certain misconception about *A Tale*. A brief consideration of why he was mistaken may bring us to a clearer understanding of what sort of account of his life Amos Oz skillfully fashioned in this book. Namdar contends that *A Tale of Love and Darkness*, unlike Oz's other books, which he sees as tightly constructed, is rambling, repetitious, and burdened with extraneous details, all of which distract from the essential subject, the mother's suicide. Namdar is then constrained to puzzle over the book's enormous popularity, and at the end of his essay, he comes up with the lame explanation that it appeals to a nostalgia for Jerusalem in the final years of the British Mandate and during the beginning of the Jewish state. That the book has spoken to millions across the globe, who surely could harbor no such nostalgia, is not mentioned.

Fania Klausner's suicide is indeed the culminating, wrenching moment of *A Tale of Love and Darkness*, but that does not mean its evocation is the ultimate purpose of the book. In his many talks and interviews about this work, Amos Oz did not make that claim. Often, as I have noted, what he said was that the book was the story of his family. That assertion requires a certain qualification. *A Tale* is the story of the formation of the writer's self as it is embedded in and emerges from the family. The lengthy sections, for example, on his mother's upbringing in Rovno, even taking the family history back a couple of generations, are important in establishing who she was and how she in turn left an indelible imprint on her son well beyond the trauma of the moment when, on a rain-swept night in Tel Aviv in her sister's apartment, she put an end to her life at the age of thirty-nine. It is the business of a novelist to work out connections in the story told—not just list one damned thing after another—and *A Tale* follows the multiple paths by which a young boy begins to define his identity against the background of both his parents and his two sets of grandparents, with their disparate families seen at earlier points in different eastern European settings. All this, moreover, is essential to Amos Oz's self-representation as a person with a vocation as a writer, which began from the moment he learned the alphabet and was able to read.

A word should also be said about the remarkable variety of tones and moods in the different episodes of this book. A life, even when marked by tragedy, is likely to encompass many aspects of comedy, of pleasure and fulfillment, of awkward and sometimes amusing mishaps, of exciting discovery, and we find all of these in *A Tale of Love and Darkness*, which is why it is such a rich reading experience, and why narrating the suicide at the end, though it casts a dark shadow over much of the story, is not its sole purpose. The jacket illustration of the original Hebrew edition is a painting from Picasso's Blue Period, *The Tragedy*, that shows, from left to right, a mother, a father, and their young son, heads bowed in sorrow, the scene rendered in gloomy blues shading into grays. But in the dedication of the copy Amos sent to me, he wrote, "This story was written in days of darkness, but within the darkness it tries to find some sparks of light." Those sparks must be accounted for together with the darkness.

Let me begin with a fraught metaphor Amos uses in the second paragraph of the book, to which he returns at later points and which has large implications as to how he viewed his life and where it would go. The opening pages of *A Tale* are a description of the apartment in Kerem Avraham where he spent his first fourteen years. It was a one-bedroom apartment, and the bedroom was his. The other room, which served as living room, dining room, study, and library, was equipped with a sofa bed that filled the space when it was opened at night. The entire basement apartment took up, he estimates, less than a hundred square feet. "A dark, narrow, slightly crooked corridor, resembling a tunnel dug by escaping prisoners, connected the kitchenette and the toilet nook to the two small rooms. A feeble bulb that was imprisoned in an iron cage cast over this corridor

even in daytime a dingy half-light[. . . .] Through a small en-
caged window our kitchen and toilet peered out on a little prison-
yard surrounded by high walls and paved in concrete." What
is striking in this description is the figurative representation of
the Klausner apartment as a prison. Everything in this constricted
space is caged, enclosed. Even the low-wattage light bulb is
"imprisoned in an iron cage." The interior corridor is like an
escape tunnel, though in the actual apartment the sense conveyed is that no one will succeed in breaking out. The yard
glimpsed through the narrow window is the yard of a prison,
with high walls that seem intended to further block escape. The
place where Amos Klausner grew up, then, is imagined as a site
of claustral incarceration. It will become his life's project to
escape—through reading, through the kibbutz, through a dedicated career as a writer that will bring his words and his vision
to vast numbers of readers, in Israel and beyond, eventually
carrying the writer himself around the world through the fame
of his books.

A further issue to address pertains to all autobiographical
writing: To what extent is the writers' representation of their
early experience an accurate register of it and to what extent
does it instead reflect the mature writers' retrospective view of
it? Determining this with any certainty is never possible. When
Amos was growing up, he may actually have felt that his childhood setting was a kind of prison, but in the book there could
also be an element of retrojection from his standpoint as a man
in his sixties, long outside Kerem Avraham and in the wide
world. After all, children often simply accept the conditions in
their immediate surroundings as a given—a child growing up in
an impoverished home doesn't necessarily perceive poverty as
long as food appears on the table. My guess is that a retrospective viewpoint is to some degree mingled with the child's actual
feelings in this narrative of the 1940s, so, as readers of the life,
we need to proceed with caution.

As for those purported digressions from the "real" story of the mother's suicide, they not only add welcome variety to the narrative but play a significant role in the development of the consciousness that will become the consciousness of the novelist. Let me illustrate with one instance. An especially entertaining episode involves the depiction of Arieh Klausner's uncle, Joseph Klausner. Most Saturdays, for three quarters of an hour, Amos and his parents would make their way by foot—there was no public transportation on Shabbat, and a taxi was beyond their means—from their tiny apartment to the spacious home, surrounded by a garden, of Uncle Joseph, located in Talpiot in the northeastern area of the Jewish section of Jerusalem.

Joseph Klausner was then an eminent figure. His 1921 book on Jesus in which, anticipating some later scholarship, he argued for the authentically Jewish character of the prophet from Nazareth, elicited wide attention. He was reviled by many as a heretic and a traitor, but the book also elicited enthusiastic responses and was translated into quite a few languages. (I wonder whether it obliquely influenced Amos in his last novel, *Judas*, which treats Judas sympathetically as the true fervent believer in Jesus's role as messiah. Judas's betrayal, then, enabled Jesus's mission of redemption. Klausner's book similarly argues for a rehabilitation of the figure of Judas.) Joseph Klausner had been appointed as the first professor of modern Hebrew literature at the newly established Hebrew University in the 1920s. He had some claim to this position, for prior to his immigration to Palestine, he had been editor of the central Hebrew literary journal in Europe, *Hashiloah*, which was published in Odessa. Though he was formidably erudite, there is some question about how legitimate a scholar he was. Before he was appointed, the university solicited an opinion from the eminent rabbinic scholar Louis Ginzberg in New York, a man of imposing intellect, who replied that Klausner was a journalist, not a scholar, so he would not recommend the appointment.

But Klausner was a man of towering egotism, as Amos's portrait of him makes vividly clear. On those Saturday afternoons around the dining room table where Amos and his parents were seated together with other guests, all carefully selected as admirers, he would hold forth in his piping little voice on a variety of topics. To right-wing Zionists like all the Klausners, some of the outpouring would be scathing denunciations of the socialist Zionists, whom he regarded as running dogs of Moscow and cowardly traitors to the national cause. His favorite topic, however, was his own work. He saw it as never having received the grand recognition it deserved, and he railed against its critics. Alternatively, he would speak of a new article he was writing that he promised would overturn received ideas and shake the intellectual world to its roots. He also harbored a certain resentment that he had been given a professorship of literature rather than history, or perhaps he even secretly expected to have been appointed in both fields. He is forgotten now, and had been for several decades before the turn of the twenty-first century, so his writing did not produce a lasting legacy. But his nephew Arieh revered him and dreamed of becoming his uncle's heir in the academic world. This never happened, and he ended up as an underling working in the National Library. His uncle would not consider helping him to a university appointment: he was afraid of being accused of nepotism, but he probably also did not have a high regard for his nephew's intellectual potential.

What is noteworthy in his great-nephew's portrait of him is that Amos studiously avoids any explicit judgmental comments, limiting himself to the lively narration of Joseph Klausner's behavior. Ultimately, he exercises what amounts to a novelist's empathetic imagination of all his characters. After the full report of Uncle Joseph's orgies of egotism at those Saturday lunches, he offers the following brief but pointed summary: "He was a good-hearted man, selfish and spoiled but sweet as a baby and arrogant as a wunderkind."

Across the street from Joseph Klausner lived S. Y. Agnon, the major Hebrew novelist of the first half of the twentieth century, destined to be awarded the Nobel Prize in Literature two decades after the Talpiot scenes reported in *A Tale of Love and Darkness*. The two men despised each other and were not on speaking terms, but the hostility between them was not symmetrical because Klausner was a self-proclaimed genius and Agnon a real one. The reasons for Klausner's dislike of Agnon were both cultural and political. Much of Agnon's work was set in the Central and Eastern Europe he had left behind, some of it dealing with modern secular Jews in Vienna or Germany, more of it engaged in the ancestral world of Jewish piety farther to the east. Agnon's use of a virtuoso Hebrew style, moreover, was a principled resistance to modernity; he deployed a matrix of the idioms, grammar, and syntax of the early rabbis with an admixture of the Hebrew of pious literature produced in more recent centuries. "My language," he said in one of his stories, "is a simple language—the language of all the generations past and all the generations to come." Joseph Klausner was repulsed by his themes and his language. He had been convinced ever since his Odessa days as an editor that the new Hebrew literature should be muscular, forthrightly modern, assertive in the national cause, liberated from the musty realm of the ghetto and all the heavy tomes of rabbinic learning, tomes that in fact lined the shelves of Agnon's study.

Not many Hebrew readers shared this hostile view of Agnon, and Arieh, as much as he revered Uncle Joseph, recognized that Agnon was a great writer. And so, at the end of the afternoon visits with Joseph Klausner, the nephew and his wife with Amos in tow would often slip across the street surreptitiously and go to see the great figure that the child Amos always referred to as

"Mr. Agnon." The novelist was invariably happy to welcome them. He treated the beautiful young mother with courtly consideration and was a friendly host to the child and his father. (Agnon could often be coy or critical with people but wasn't with these visitors, and he seems to have kept in check the sly self-regard he often exhibited to others.) Amos's metaphorical representation of Agnon is memorable and catches something essential about him both as a person and as a writer who cultivated subtle ambiguities in his work.

> Whenever Mr. Agnon would rise from his place and go over to pull out from one of his shelves one volume or another— the books seemed like a congregation of crowded worshippers in dark attire, a little shabby—his image would cast around it not one shadow but two or three shadows, or even more. That was how his image was incised in my childhood memory, and that is how I remember him to this day: a man moving in dim lights and three or four different shadows moving with him as he went, in front of him, to his right, behind him, above him, and beneath his feet.

The deployment of multiple shadows as they evidently struck the boy's imagination is a small instance of the way Amos's report of his childhood memories is a novelist's richly imagined representation of character and scene.

As an adult, though he was not close to Agnon, he occasionally visited him, and later on, as a professor at Ben-Gurion University, he often taught Agnon's fiction, with his teaching leading in 1997 to an excellent critical book, *The Silence of the Heavens*, on Agnon's modernist masterpiece, *Only Yesterday*. He also recognized, however, that there was something dangerously seductive for him as a writer in Agnon's artfully cunning, finely rhythmic, subtly archaizing prose, and he attests that he fought for years to liberate himself from it and not to emulate it inadvertently. The danger might have been especially tempting for him because, as he asserted in one of his talks, the Hebrew language was his lifelong addiction, the one cause about which he would never compromise. That addiction began with the exotic and fascinating Hebrew to which he was first exposed by his early teacher, Zelda Schneurson, and afterward at the religious school to which his secular parents decided to send him: "My heart was drawn to the decorous combinations, to the almost totally forgotten words, to the strange syntactic configurations, and to the remote regions in the thicket of the language's forest, places where no human had trod for hundreds of years, to the fine-honed beauty of the Hebrew language." His impulse to stylistic abundance led him to writing that differed from the rigorously understated prose Agnon cultivated after the effusiveness of his earliest fiction. In any case, Amos felt he had to be careful not to be drawn into the alluring model of the manifestly archaic Hebrew created by Agnon, yet he reveled in the intrinsic stylistic resources of his native language, incorporating some of its earlier strata in much of his writing. His mustering of the expressive resources of the Hebrew language is partly what makes *A Tale of Love and Darkness* such a remarkable telling of the story of his childhood.

Among all the abundance of things told in *A Tale* about Amos's childhood there are also things untold, either by calculated choice or by simple dismissal because they seemed extraneous. His earliest years were spent against the background of a world in upheaval. The Second World War began the same year he was born. He was too young to be aware that in 1942 Rommel was advancing toward Egypt and threatening to conquer Palestine, which would have led to the slaughter of its Jewish population, a grim menace that was palpable for the Jews of the country but was averted by the British defeat of the German forces at El Alamein. But by the time Amos was four, even before he could read, he became absorbed in the advance and retreat of armies across the European continent, marked in maps published in the daily press, maps that as still a little boy he managed to follow. His widow, Nily Oz, goes so far as to attribute his lifelong engagement in the political realm and in the relevance of politics to territory—a relevance crucial in the ongoing conflict in Israel-Palestine—to his precocious map reading. Very little was known of the Nazi genocide in the *yishuv*, the Zionist community in Palestine, during much of the war, and Amos, turning six at the war's end, could not have learned of it till some years after. He makes a few fairly brief references to the Shoah, the Holocaust, in the book, but it surely came to cast a deep shadow over his consciousness: he would discover that almost all of his mother's family who had remained in Rovno were murdered by the Nazis, as well as many friends and beloved teachers from her Tarbut school. Amos never wrote fiction that was directly about the genocide, but his haunting novella *Crusade*—the Hebrew title, *Unto Death*, is more apt—about a band of Crusaders struggling across Europe to reach the Holy Land while driven by the mad obsession of finding and destroying the hidden Jew in their midst, is a displacement onto the Middle Ages of the mindset impelling the modern mass killers.

The most prominent public event that affected the young Amos was the decision of the U.N. General Assembly on November 29, 1947, to partition Palestine into a Jewish state and an Arab state. On that night, the Klausners took their eight-year-old son out into the streets, where crowds from the neighborhood had gathered, to listen to the radios of the few who possessed them as the voting in the General Assembly took place. When a majority was reached for partition, there was jubilation in the streets, a moment Amos would not forget. But the jubilation was followed in the days afterward by artillery barrages from the Jordanian side directed at the Jewish neighborhoods of Jerusalem, and these would continue through most of the ensuing war.

All this is duly recorded in *A Tale of Love and Darkness*, but Amos chooses not to register the terror he must at times have felt during the attacks. Compounding the daily bombardments, Arab Legion snipers, well trained by the British, targeted whomever they were able to bring into their sights in the western part of the city. A ten-year-old boy, the child of a couple the Klausners knew, just a bit older than Amos, was shot and killed while playing outside. A woman with whom the Klausner family was friendly was gunned down while hanging out laundry to dry. There were in all likelihood other killings of which the young Amos would have been aware. In a brief reflection on Jerusalem, "Alien City," written just a few weeks after the conclusion of the Six-Day War in 1967, he recalls how he, a nine-year-old, saw a man lying in the street who had been killed by a Jordanian shell, his belly ripped apart by it, and how that sight haunted his nights. Perhaps because this brief piece was framed for inclusion in *Soldiers Talk*, a volume of conversations about the experience of confronting the mayhem of war that Amos co-edited, he felt it appropriate to incorporate this grisly detail. But he made a strategic decision not to include such things in *A Tale of Love and Darkness*.

The material conditions during the fighting were dreadful. The besieged Jewish part of Jerusalem was being both shelled and locked down. Friends and neighbors moved into the tiny Klausner apartment, for they thought its basement location made it relatively safe from the bombardment. At least twenty-five people took refuge with the Klausners. It is very hard to imagine how all these could have crammed into those hundred square feet, even with mattresses piled on the floor in every available space. (Perhaps the twenty-five were not all there simultaneously.) Food was also in short supply; it was mainly brought in to Jerusalem by armed convoys that made their way under fire up the steep winding road from the coastal plain. In Amos's account, the hardships and the fears of this dire situation are given scant expression. Instead, he writes of the excitement and the sense of duty fulfilled in racing through the streets to carry out errands for the defense forces. His narrative reflects a general inclination he would continue to manifest: not to dwell on horrors he may have experienced or of which he was aware. Thus the slaughter of cousins and other relatives in Rovno is just briefly stated, and as we saw, he chose not to undertake a direct imaginative engagement with the Nazi genocide in his fiction. Similarly, he saw some terrible things on the battlefield in 1967 and 1973 but was silent about them in his writing, only twice, in a late interview and in a recorded conversation, responding in troubling sensory detail to a question about his experience at the front. Perhaps as a staunchly rational liberal, he thought it best to focus on humane solutions for problems of the present because brooding on past horrors might lead instead to impulses of hatred and vengeance. But he may have also felt a self-protective emotional motive to avert his gaze from all horrors, just as he did for so long with his mother's suicide.

Another, very different kind of gap in Amos's story of his childhood has to do with his precociousness. Though he certainly does not hide the fact that he was in general a good student, he probably sensed that emphasizing any early signs of unusual intellectual ability was unseemly. After he deciphered maps showing the progress of the war when he was four, he acquired the rudiments of the ability to read, which he did by the age of five, before he was taught to read in school. Once he could read, he seated himself in front of his father's little Hebrew-keyboard Olivetti and typed the following words, with the intention of placing the sheet on a wall or door: *Amos Klausner sofer*, "Amos Klausner author." Books, literature, writing pervaded the basement apartment. His mother was a devoted reader until her depression reached the point where she could only sit and stare. His father, with his dream of establishing himself as a scholar, spent long hours at his desk, reference works and primary literary sources stacked around him, indefatigably taking notes and writing. He would not complete a doctorate until the early 1960s, in London, on Y. L. Peretz, an important figure in Hebrew literary history in its European phase. Writing was complemented with storytelling by Amos's mother. She told strange, often spooky tales abounding in witches in dark forests, menacing trolls, black magic; and the stories she told her young son about the Rovno of her girlhood were equally somber: she did not shrink from tales of fatal infidelities and tragic suicides. This may not have been a recommended curriculum for a small boy, but clearly Fania Klausner made Amos a writer in these ways, even in some instances inviting him to collaborate with her in the oral invention of the tales she told. The somber side of much of his fiction surely derives in part from her brooding narratives of spectral presences.

Storytelling quickly became an important social resource for him. He was not a robust or athletic child, nor did he become any more vigorous when he moved to the kibbutz or then when he served in the army. Perhaps inevitably, stronger boys at school were tempted to pick on the perceived weakling, but Amos hit on a strategy for warding off bullying: he would spin out stories to tell the other boys, stories that they found spellbinding, inducing them to gather around and listen and then to await the next installment. This neutralization of hostility from his schoolmates might be described as Amos's first author's fee.

In any event, he was discovering at this very early age that what he wanted to be and needed to be was a writer. This sense of vocation would stay with him all his life. Though he would achieve both fame and ample remuneration through his writing, success that must have been very gratifying, he did not write chiefly to be famous or to outshine other writers—though those may well have been among his motives—but to do what he had to do in the world. That inner drive began when he was five, six, and seven. I would like to follow its ramifications here in a crucial passage of *A Tale of Love and Darkness*. The portentous poetic emphasis manifested throughout the recounting of this moment reflects the importance he felt it had in his life story.

To propose the "real" subject of a book as multifaceted as *A Tale* may be imprudent, but I want to do that now. Its subject is not, let me say, something Amos himself mentioned in any of his talks or interviews about the book. All this teeming abundance of different episodes—the history of his mother's family, the Mossmans, the portrait of the paternal grandparents and their odd marriage, Teacher Zelda and her idiosyncratic tutelage of the boy, the shabby surroundings of the neighborhood, the mother's storytelling and even her suicide—are the shaping elements from which the writer Amos Oz was to emerge.

Chapter 33 concludes with a passage too long to quote except in an excerpt that pulls much of this, and more, together. The six-year-old Amos is lying on his back on the concrete surface of one of those bare courtyards of Kerem Avraham, looking up at the sky as evening gradually descends. His senses are acutely attuned to everything around him: the laundry hanging on roofs, the scrawny alley cats, the changing colors of the sky, a neighborhood girl hesitantly sounding out on a piano the initial bars of Beethoven's "Für Elise," to which a bird answers, as another bird will be imagined with those same notes when Fania Klausner puts an end to her life at the book's conclusion. The six-year-old experiences a kind of ecstasy as he takes all this in, evoked through the richest resources of a lyric Hebrew to which no translation can do full justice, and in that ecstasy, he perceives a moral imperative. I will pick up the passage at a middle point.

> It was as though the valley of the shadow of death were yawning wide and being laid bare in the heavens, as though the heavens were not up there, with the one lying on his back beneath them, but now the reverse, the whole sky was an abyss

and the one on his back was no longer lying but hovering—
tucked in and quickly sinking and dropping like a stone toward the velvet ground below. You—this evening you must
never forget: you are only six or barely six and a half, but for
the first time in your little life there is something tremen-
dous and fearful in what has opened before you, something
serious, grim-faced, something stretching out from endlessness to endlessness, and it's come upon you, and it's a mute
giant, and it penetrates and suddenly opens up all of you so
that you too are as though wider and deeper than yourself,
and in a voice that is not yours but is perhaps the voice you
will have when thirty or forty years have passed, in a voice
that brooks neither laughter nor frivolity, it commands you
not to forget, never to forget a single detail of this evening's
details: remember and keep its smells, remember its body and
its light, remember its birds and the notes of the piano and
the cries of the crows and all the strangeness of the sky that
came about before your eyes from horizon to horizon, and
all of them for you, and all of them for the eyes of the ad-
dressee only.

The passage goes on to enumerate all the elements of the scene
and the child's recollections that must never be forgotten—
passersby and family members and the taste of foods—ending
in a spectacular verbal evocation of the colors of the evening and
the sound of the piano playing "Für Elise," with the answering
song of the bird.

This moving moment is a rite of dedication of the small
boy as an artist imbued with the uncompromising imperative
to listen, see, smell, taste, and touch the world around him, ab-
sorb it, find ways to get it into words. The moment is akin to
Stephen Dedalus's determination in *A Portrait of the Artist as a
Young Man* "to encounter for the millionth time the reality of
experience and to forge in the smithy of my soul the uncreated
conscience of my race." *A Tale of Love and Darkness* is before all
else, let me propose, Amos Oz's portrait of the artist as a young

boy. Everything in the book makes up that portrait—the craziness of some of his relatives, his eccentric schooling, the many odd types he encounters in Kerem Avraham, the family history in Europe, his parents' strained relationship, his mother's love for him with all those stories she told him and her forever wounding abandonment of him when he was still scarcely more than a child. If there is an inner circle to all these circumambient pieces of experience pressing on him, it is his parents. What happens with them and through them in Amos's early years and beyond needs to be explored in detail.

Amos never asks how this disparate couple came together. Perhaps he preferred not to broach the subject. Fania Mossman had been in Palestine only half a year when she met Yehuda Arieh Klausner. He could hardly have struck her as the bold and manly hero of a girl's typical romantic fantasies, so maybe his learning had some role in her being drawn to him. She was, after all, a woman who cherished the realm of books, and even in this time of upheaval she had no doubts about committing herself to a university education, first in Prague and then in Jerusalem. In the unfamiliar new reality of Palestine she was clearly disoriented and insecure, cut loose from her cultural moorings in Europe, and an erudite young man seemingly headed toward an academic future may well have seemed like a safe haven. He on his part would readily have been allured by her beauty, and perhaps he thought that her romantic literary bent would be the perfect complement to his more scholarly engagement in the realm of literature. As their marriage unfolded through the thirteen years till its abrupt and violent conclusion, all calculations of this sort proved to be woefully mistaken.

Fania and Arieh Klausner were never what I would call estranged from each other. There were no open clashes, no shouting matches, and they continued to treat each other with consideration, sympathy, even compassion. But they inhabited two different planets on diverging orbits that inexorably moved further apart. One passage in *A Tale of Love and Darkness* summarizes the essential disparities between husband and wife. After noting his father's, "Abba's," impulse to talk and talk, Amos draws a sharp contrast between his parents:

> He commanded an imposing range of knowledge while she was keen-eyed and at times saw into the heart. He was straightforward and rigorous and decent and diligent, while she was always looking to understand why whoever maintained a particular view clung especially to that view and not to another and why the person who vehemently disagreed with the one who held the first view had such a piercing need to cling in particular to the opposite view. Clothes interested her only as a window into the inner world of those who wore them. When she would sit in the home of acquaintances, she would always attend scrupulously to the upholstery, the curtains, the sofas, the mementos scattered across the window sills, and the ornamental toys on the shelves while all the others were immersed in debate—as though she had been assigned some sort of detective mission. People's secrets always fascinated her, but when the conversation turned to gossip, she would listen with her faint smile, a hesitant smile that seemed self-dismissive, and she would remain silent. But if she emerged from her silence and spoke a few sentences, the conversation was no longer what it had been before she spoke.
>
> When Abba spoke to her, one would sometimes detect in his voice a certain mingling of cowardice and distance and affection and respect and fear—as if he had in his home a fortune-teller with a false identity. Or a necromancer.

After this detailed evocation of the mother's strange social presence and the way she saw people, Amos's brief notation about his father's response to his wife is telling. It was by no means alienation but rather a sense of being daunted, a little frightened, and mystified by an imposing presence that he could never penetrate or understand. This incomprehension was surely not the ultimate cause of Fania Klausner's growing depression, but it must have magnified her feeling of isolation and in this way exacerbated her depression.

Knowing the actual cause of her condition is not possible. It could even have been a congenital chemical imbalance. In any case, the disruption of her familiar world in the flight to Palestine; then, after the defeat of Germany, news of the mass slaughter in Rovno that cut down so many people dear to her; and perhaps the constant burden of maintaining a household in impoverished circumstances after having grown up in affluence— all were likely contributors to her gradual, then precipitous, decline.

What effect might such a troubled, strangely magnetic mother have had on her young son? It is obvious that her presence set him on the path to become a novelist, not only in the storytelling she shared with him but, as the passage we just considered suggests, in her predisposition to look into the inwardness of people, to ponder their motives, to pick up clues about them from clothes and furnishings and knickknacks. He carried out in writing what she could not do: "My mother, so it seems to me, wanted me to grow up and express instead of her what was not granted her to express." Amos as a child manifestly identified with his mother rather than with his father and was much closer to her. The closeness made her sudden abandonment of her child when she ended her own life all the more shattering. That scene of abandonment never altogether left him. He would create fictional surrogates for both his parents in several of his novels and novellas. The two most memorable instances are in his breakout novel of 1968, *My Michael,* in which the rational, diligent, altogether square husband, Michael, is incapable of fathoming his emotionally disturbed wife, Hannah, from whose perspective the story is pointedly told, and then in the striking novella of 1976, *The Hill of Evil Counsel,* which, set in 1946, centers on a similar couple, with the mother, at the end, fleeing eastward to parts unknown with a British admiral and abandoning her young son. To be entirely cautious, let me add that Amos's unquestioning lifelong conviction that his mother committed suicide might just possibly have been wrong: desperately tormented by insomnia, she might have unintentionally overdosed on her sleeping pills, a possibility whose likelihood no one can now determine.

In young Amos's formative years, his mother's steep decline was a continuous trial. It began when he was eight. From that point on, she was no longer there despite being physically present. Racked by her acute insomnia, for which the prescribed medications gave her imperfect relief at best or no relief at all, she sat in a chair staring blankly out the window, no longer reading, virtually paralyzed by her mental illness. The utter bleakness of her life lends credence to the assumption, invariably Amos's, that she deliberately ended things by suicide. The sight of her in this dire condition must have been agonizing to the young child. At one point in his account of his mother's withdrawal from the world, he reports being angry with her for being absent, which is understandable, as is his initial surge of anger at her suicide. During the four years of her virtual absence as she sat in that chair, the father and his young son were constrained to shoulder the full responsibility of managing the little household: they took turns at preparing meals and doing the marketing. Amos had school to attend, and the father had his work at the library, so it was not easy for them to keep up with things, nor was either particularly well equipped to handle the domestic tasks. They somehow got along, but the home fell into disarray, dishes piled up in the sink, dirt was everywhere. Amos's distress with this situation carried over into adult life as a need to have everything around him tidy and in neat order: no mess tolerated. Creating fiction would have been another way of imposing order, for in the best circumstances, the writer can set everything in its proper place and pull all the disparate strands of a story into an overarching imaginative coherence.

At the age of twelve and a half, then, Amos lost his mother. At the age of fourteen and a half he definitively parted company from his father, becoming a kind of orphan, which is how his future wife, Nily, perceived him when he arrived at Kibbutz Hulda. He, on his part, uses the word "foundling" (*asufi*) to describe himself at a late moment in *A Tale of Love and Darkness*. His choice of that term rather than "orphan" (*yatom*) has an interesting implication: the foundling, taken in by the couple who discovers him, is raised to assume a different identity from the one he would have had if brought up by his biological parents.

Amos's separation from his father had a political aspect, and that needs to be explained. The Klausners were all Revisionist Zionists, adherents of the right-wing Herut party, on which the later Likud party would be built. The Herut members were not Jewish fascists, as their detractors claimed, but they adhered to a militant kind of Zionism, abhorred the collectivism of the Zionist Left, and were territorial maximalists. The party's rousing anthem, its words written by the party's moving spirit, Zev Jabotinsky, begins with the lines: "Two banks has the Jordan, / this one is ours and the other, too." The leader of the party at the time of the founding of the State of Israel was Menachem Begin. In 1977, with the erosion of the Israeli Left, he would become prime minister. The boy Amos idolized Begin, imagining him as a hero of national liberation—bold, muscular, physically and morally robust. When he first laid eyes on the great leader at the age of ten, Amos was taken aback: the actual Begin was pale and fragile-looking, his facial features those of a stereotypical ghetto Jew, this general effect reinforced by his large round spectacles. But the rhetoric he deployed in his speeches was fiery.

The chasm between Left and Right in Israeli politics at that time, as it would continue to be, was far wider than a disagreement over policies. Each side despised and demonized the other, a state of affairs that unfortunately would become familiar in American politics after the presidential election of 2016. Uncle Joseph's fierce denunciations of socialist Zionism at those Saturday lunches were typical of the mood and attitude prevalent in Herut circles. Amos's familiarity with ideological fanaticism at an early age would play a significant role both in his fiction and in his political views. He understood how people could be utterly consumed with ideological fervor. Even as his own politics moved decisively to the Left, he was able to create in his fiction compelling portraits of intransigent ideological militants, many of them rightists, more effectively than any other Israeli writer. Indeed, his striking ability to represent figures whose values were abhorrent to him is one of the hallmarks of his gift as a novelist. The phenomenon of political fanaticism troubled him, for he was deeply convinced that reasonableness and an open mind should inform political thinking; late in life, he wrote a small book addressing this issue, *Dear Zealot.*

When Amos was ten, his Klausner grandfather, no doubt with the intention of inspiring the boy and furthering his political education, took him one Saturday morning to a Herut rally held in the Edison movie theater in downtown Jerusalem. The grandfather and the child were seated near the front of the crowded hall: Menachem Begin himself was to deliver the principal address to the rapt audience of his followers. The child's first disappointment was the physical appearance of the man he had idolized. More disappointment followed.

What ensued as Begin spoke was hilarious, but unfortunately the hilarity of the moment is not amenable to translation because it turns on a matter of Hebrew usage. Begin had learned his rather stiff, formal Hebrew in Poland and was not in touch with the new version of the language spoken in the streets, with which Amos was perfectly familiar. As Begin's rousing speech rose to a crescendo, he invoked the despicable act of all the great powers in arming the Arab states while he denounced the cowardly failure of response by the socialist government led by David Ben-Gurion. The verb he used for "to arm," *lezayen*, is derived from a good biblical term, *zayin*, which in the ancient language means "weapon." Hebrew, however, had moved on. In Israeli slang, *zayin* had come to be a rude word for the penis, and the transitive verb derived from it was used out on the streets in the sense of "to fuck." (This transfer of the original meaning might be parallel to the etymology of the English term, which scholars surmise derives from a verb that means "to strike.") So when Begin, with fever-pitch oratorical anaphora, complained that one power after another was arming the Arabs, that "the whole world day and night was arming our Arab enemies," and concluded, "Were I now prime minister, all of them, every one of them, would be arming us!," what the young Amos as a native speaker of Israeli Hebrew heard was that every one of them would be performing a coarsely sexual act on us, an act not gauged to fortify Israel's military posture. The ten-year-old could not contain himself: he burst into uncontrollable laughter, scandalizing his grandfather and whoever in the packed hall heard the peals of laughter. The grandfather grabbed him by the ear and hauled him out of the auditorium. This was the definitive moment, Amos asserts, when he broke forever with right-wing Zionism.

The boy's disillusionment with the ideology on which he had been nurtured and which had inflamed his imagination was triggered by a matter of language. All his life, he would be devoted to the task of finding exactly the right words to represent his characters, their world, and his own views about politics, his country's predicaments, human nature, and history. For the leader of a party to be ignorant of what had become of the language that he needed to use struck the child as a lack of connection between the promoted ideology and what was going on in the real world. Inflated terms, the ringing enunciation of words with meanings of which the speaker himself was ignorant, suggested to the boy that the angry pitch of militant Zionism was no more than a farrago of high-sounding, empty phrases. This is how, the author of *A Tale* hyperbolically claims, Amos Klausner became a socialist. The actual process no doubt took longer, but less than five years later, it would culminate in his departure for a kibbutz.

The political comedy at the Edison theater is counter-pointed at the end of *A Tale of Love and Darkness* by the tragedy of the mother's suicide. What Amos was clearly driven to do in writing about the most painful event in his life was to swing around 180 degrees from the way he had coped with it, or rather not coped with it, for half a century. He had not breathed a word about it in all that time, even though he must have been aware that others knew of it. In those two years of aching emptiness in the little basement apartment after his mother's death, neither he nor his father, who was complicit with him in the silence, ever spoke about it. For years he never touched on his mother's suicide, not even with his wife or with his daughters. Then, as he entered his sixties, in a decision that would have required some moral courage, he decided to imagine his mother's last hours with his full resources as a novelist, to plot the exact course of her last walk through the darkened streets of Tel Aviv on a rainy night, to record every detail up to the moment when she swallowed the lethal quantity of sleeping pills. In his imagining of the terrible moment, he fantasizes being present in the room, knocking the pills away, tying her hands so she cannot carry out the act. Then he conjures up the ambulance that rushes the comatose Fania Klausner to a hospital, too late to save her. That bird singing the first notes of "Für Elise" recurs at the very end of the book, trying futilely to waken with song the irrevocably dead woman: "and still sometimes it tries." Thus a resonant, thoroughly novelistic invention ends *A Tale of Love and Darkness.*

Somewhat earlier in the book, Amos convincingly records his shifting reactions as a twelve-year-old to what he was sure was the suicide. His initial reflex was a wave of anger: "I was angry with her that she had taken off, with no farewell, no hug, no word of explanation." A few weeks later, the anger yielded to a sense of guilt: "the more I ceased to hate my mother, the more I began to despise myself." If only he had been a better kid, if only he hadn't tossed his clothes on the floor, muddied the kitchen with his dirty shoes, pestered her, if only he had been a more sociable and less reclusive child, she wouldn't have killed herself. A related sense of guilt would persist till the end of his life. A little after her death, it occurred to him that if his mother had abandoned him in this way, so abruptly, then she had never really loved him. He continued to struggle with these conflicting feelings as an adult; as he was dying, he was still plagued by them. We have to conclude that any catharsis he achieved in finally writing about his mother's death was only partial and temporary.

The spookiest imagining of his mother's suicide, in which he enters into the gothic world of dark woods and menacing supernatural beings that populated the tales she told him, is that death was a seductive lover who lured her into betraying her husband and her child. "It was something that led my mother, since life had not fulfilled a single one of the promises of her youth, to imagine death in the image of a rousing lover who was also both provocative and soothing, an ultimate lover, a lover-muse who at last would heal the wounds of her solitary heart." This troubling fantasy prompts the narrator to say that for years he has been following the footsteps of "this aged murderer, this ancient canny seducer [. . .], this hunter of broken hearts, this vampire-suitor whose voice is bittersweet like the muffled sound of a cello on lonely nights, a velvet, subtle schemer, artist of plots, magic flutist who draws into the folds of his silken robe the lonely and the despairing." Long before he wrote this book,

Amos had cast death as a seducer in the guise of that British admiral who persuades the mother of the boy in *The Hill of Evil Counsel* to run away with him.

The two years in which father and son lived together, often not speaking, in the apartment in which there was no longer a wife and mother must have been a dreadful time for Amos as he entered adolescence, though he says very little about it in the book. The need to break out of that prisonlike place would surely have mounted in him during those long months. His move to a kibbutz was at once an escape from the confines of the apartment and the bleak memories it harbored, an escape from Kerem Avraham, an escape from the father who had become no more than the estranged sharer of a burden, and an escape from the insistent rightist clamoring of the Klausners. The question that is addressed only by implication in *A Tale of Love and Darkness* is what sort of lasting imprint the felt incarceration, together with the trauma of the mother's suicide, left on Amos Klausner after he became Amos Oz, how all of it shaped him as a person. He would, let me propose, live his life on two levels. Though he was deeply wounded by much that happened in his early years, even before the disappearance of his mother, Amos was endowed with great gifts, and he would use them as resources for very successfully getting along in the world. Despite his anxiety about being pale and weak, he was extraordinarily good-looking as a child, as an adolescent, and as a grown man. He was intellectually brilliant, with the kind of intelligence not limited to performing in the classroom but involving a keen, level-headed understanding of what was going on between people and what was happening in the political realm. He had an almost preternatural facility with language, accompanied by a gift for storytelling. And as time went on, it became clear that he could charm audiences.

All of these attributes made the public Amos and the social Amos confident and poised, engaging, considerate of others, and many people saw him that way. The wounds of childhood, however, had not really healed, and it is not in the least an exaggeration to say that they festered all his life. The subterranean self of the genuinely accomplished and socially adept Amos persisted in that "foundling," abandoned and alone in the world. *A Tale of Love and Darkness* might be viewed as a sustained effort to exorcise the subterranean self of what had so long haunted it. But the haunting had gone on for many years, never really relenting; it let him fathom, and brought him in his fiction to express, the dark side of the mind and heart. After a first generation of Israeli writers disposed to imagine men and women chiefly as social creatures—in peer groups, in the army, on the kibbutz—Amos wrote novels and stories that penetrated the condition of isolates, who were often struggling with private demons. He brought a new note to Hebrew writing, one that would resonate with readers far beyond the constrictive borders of the Jewish state.

2

—•◆•—

The Kibbutz, Romance, and the Army

AT THE AGES of thirteen and fourteen, Amos was a student in the *gymnasia*—in Hebrew this is a feminine singular term meaning "secondary school," *gymnasium* being the European equivalent—of Rehavia, one of Jerusalem's most prestigious high schools, located in the affluent neighborhood of Rehavia in the western part of the city, where a good many of the homes were occupied by professors at the Hebrew University. But emotionally shaken by his mother's suicide, he was uncharacteristically incapable of focusing on his studies. This, then, was a kind of liminal period for the adolescent Amos. Life in the little apartment with his father continued to be unrelentingly bleak. His recent commitment to the socialist version of Zionism crystallized in these two years, in defiance of the political environment in which he had grown up, and he would remain faithful to the socialist ideal for the rest of his life. Aching to escape from the carceral enclosure of his home and also from the Kerem Avra-

31

ham neighborhood, he declared to his father that he wanted to move to a kibbutz. This could scarcely have pleased Arieh Klausner, loyal as he and his extended family were to the Herut party and to Jabotinsky's vision of Zionism, which regarded socialism as anathema, but when he realized how resolute his son was, he grudgingly conceded. He had remarried not very long after his wife's death, in all likelihood to the woman he had been meeting in Jerusalem cafés as the incapacitated Fania sat in her chair, blankly staring. The young Amos, much to the child's distress, had discovered the liaison while walking with a friend through downtown Jerusalem. He did not want to have much to do with his stepmother, and he was disinclined to have a continuing engagement with his unforthcoming father, now married to another woman. His father was no doubt relieved not to have to deal further with his resentful young son. The company of father and son had become a burden to both.

The first step in Amos's departure was a temporary placement during the summer of 1953 in a kibbutz in the north, chosen by his father because it was located in proximity to some family members. For a more long-term place for the boy, his father chose Kibbutz Hulda, down in the coastal plain, because there it was possible to obtain a baccalaureate degree, *bagrut*, which was a prerequisite for higher education. Whatever the political and emotional chasm between Amos and his father, Arieh Klausner wanted his son to be able to get a university education: that was a bedrock value for him.

Hulda is less than thirty-five miles from Jerusalem, but for the fourteen-and-a-half-year-old Amos, it was a journey to the antipodes. He who had lived as an only child in a little basement apartment with his own bedroom now had to accustom himself to collective living, to sleeping in a large room, a kind of dormitory, with a whole group of boys his age, many of whom were not especially friendly toward him, including those in the bunks adjacent to his. After his cloistered existence in Jerusalem surrounded at home by piles of books, he was working out in the fields, something to which he had aspired as a budding Labor Zionist but which he found physically and psychologically challenging. Amos repeatedly said that he had dreamed of turning himself into a suntanned, muscular, vigorous kibbutznik, but he had remained, he wryly added, the pale, unathletic, bookish child of Kerem Avraham, visible to all even beneath his acquired tan. The self-assessment was accurate: even as he conscientiously did his agricultural work, he was not athletic, not physically vigorous, still caught up in books and writing, and was perceived by his peers on the kibbutz as a someone who didn't belong.

Entering the kibbutz before the age of fifteen—initially as an "external" resident, not yet a member—was in one way a throwback to the experience of many boys that age half a century earlier, when a male in his mid-teens was thought of as an adult and could be allowed to head to America alone from Eastern Europe in the great wave of Jewish immigration. But Amos was not joining a larger movement of migration: he came alone to an unfamiliar world, and some time would pass before he could find his way beyond the loneliness. Another element of the shock of coming to Hulda, which he reported in a late recorded conversation, came from leaving the dour ascetic realm of Jerusalem and entering a place where the girls wore very tight short shorts and similarly tight T-shirts, affording a vista of permissiveness and sexual allure that at first seemed quite beyond his reach.

A significant element of this moment of transition for Amos was his decision to change his last name. The implications of that change are clear, but they deserve reviewing and amplification. In the 1950s, the first decade of statehood, there was a general drive in Israel, encouraged by Ben-Gurion, to replace names originating in languages of the Diaspora with Hebrew names. In some cases, people chose Hebrew names that sounded a little like their original names, but the most common practice

was to opt for a Hebrew translation. Thus, Stein ("stone") became Even, the Hebrew word for "stone," and Eisen ("iron") or
"Eisenberg" was transformed into Barzel (the Hebrew word
for "iron") or Barzilai. Amos Klausner did something different.
Klausner in German means "recluse." I'm not sure Amos was
aware of that meaning, though it would have had a degree of
appropriateness for his lonely life alongside his father in their
Jerusalem apartment. He had moved now into a collective but
was still a loner. *Oz* is the Hebrew word for "strength" and even
has some association in the Bible with military strength. It is
what Amos aspired to possess, along with the suntan. It is also
a compact monosyllabic word that almost *sounds* strong and has
the advantage of alliterating with his first name. (In Hebrew,
both names begin with the same letter, *ayin*.)

The replacement of his original name was, of course, a declaration of separation from the whole extended Klausner family and their adherence to right-wing ideology, but, above all,
it announced a sharp divide from his father, Arieh Klausner. In
fact, his father was deeply hurt by this renunciation of his last
name. Their separation was enacted in deed when Amos came
to Hulda. Not long after, his father went to England for an
eight-year stay with his new wife, where they would have two
children and where, at long last, he would manage to complete
a Ph.D. in Hebrew literature, albeit too late in life to facilitate
any move from the position he had held as mere librarian to the
long-dreamed-of academic career. Arieh Klausner's second wife
was quite wealthy, so there would have been no problem with
material support during his years of doctoral work in England.
His visits to Israel, and to Amos, were infrequent during this
period, as well as mutually unsatisfying, and would continue
to be very infrequent after his return to Israel. The adolescent,
moreover, had scant opportunity while living on the kibbutz to
establish any intimacy with his half-siblings, even had he wanted
to. Amos's alienation from his father eventually moderated. After

Arieh Klausner died at the age of sixty, Amos edited a book of his articles, and the tone he took in his introduction to the volume is respectful, even reverential. The work was a gesture toward making amends for the bad feelings between father and son through the years of his youth.

Though Amos, in his mid-teens, aspired to separate from his father, the sense of being abandoned by his father was quite another matter, and that is essentially what happened. Not only did Arieh Klausner go off to England with a new family, but he even stopped sending payment for clothing for his son, evidently because he did not realize it was required for nonmember residents of the kibbutz (or perhaps he chose not to realize it). Amos's feelings of not being part of things were thus compounded by going around in frayed garments and shoes with holes in the soles. Nily Zuckerman, daughter of the kibbutz librarian, who at the age of twenty would marry Amos, says that she saw him as an orphan from the beginning and continued to feel that he remained a kind of orphan as time passed. Certain private remarks Amos would make over the years suggest that he shared this sense.

Those early months on the kibbutz were extremely difficult for him, and he was lonely and almost desperate at times. Yet he gradually began to make connections with some people there that mitigated his sense of isolation. Many of the boys his age viewed him as an oddball and, with the cruelty often exhibited by the young, were altogether unwelcoming; they taunted him, played tricks on him, even sometimes beat him. All this, he said in a talk celebrating Nily's sixtieth birthday, he accepted as merely what he deserved because he *did* feel inferior to these healthy, happy, vigorous young people.

The acceptance of his misery as appropriate punishment did not, however, dull the sharp pain caused by the humiliation and taunts inflicted by his peers. Late in life, he expressed remorse over having allowed his daughters to suffer during their time in the kibbutz by living in the children's quarters. (His son, because he was subject to attacks of asthma, was taken by his parents from the children's house at the age of eighteen months and brought to stay with them in their little kibbutz apartment.) The terms in which Amos admitted to his feelings of guilt over leaving the girls in the children's quarters are shockingly extreme: collective existence in the children's house, as he saw it, was not just a trial but at times a nightmare. The vehemence he used is so emphatic that I am compelled to conclude that he was not only thinking about his daughters but also remembering his own experience as an adolescent. Amos had thought that breaking away from the claustral world of his Jerusalem childhood by moving to the kibbutz would be a liberation, but, as an often scorned outsider, he discovered he had gone from one kind of misery to another, at least with many of the boys his age. The loneliness and isolation of his early years continued to plague him in a new guise.

Eventually Amos did make friends with at least a couple of the kibbutz boys, though, alas, no one with a bed near his in that housing for teenagers. One older kibbutznik, Oyzer Huldai, took him under his wing, acting as a mentor and becoming his friend. There was on the kibbutz a mechanism for "adopting" children who had come there without parents—not a legal adoption but a way of designating a particular couple as the stand-in family within the kibbutz community for the young person arrived from the outside. Oyzer Huldai and his wife chose not to adopt Amos like this, but they nevertheless were a comforting and reassuring presence for him in his new setting, and he continued to express warm feelings for them as time went on.

Amos, even as he yearned to become a muscular worker of the soil, remained the same aspiring literary person who as a five-year-old had typed out that proclamation of identity, "Amos Klausner author." While a child in Jerusalem, he had written poems, as early as the age of ten, some of which he showed to

Teacher Zelda. He had also handwritten a one-page newspaper that he made available to other children to read and return for the price of one *grush*. (A grush, the least valuable coin in the monetary system of those years, would have been worth rather less than a penny.) At the age of thirteen and a half, a year after his mother's death, he wrote a short piece on the loss of a mother for *Haaretz Shelanu*, a newspaper for children. When he came to Hulda a year later, in the midst of visions of himself wielding a hoe, plowing fields, and milking cows, he was just as driven as ever to write, even though he knew the activity, in which none of his peers was engaged, could easily have triggered mockery. In fact, for a time he felt writing was shameful, something done in secret, like masturbation. His earliest mode of writing at Hulda, when he was turning out melancholy poems, was therefore more or less clandestine. When he moved on to writing short stories, no doubt sensing they were a little less shameful than poetry, and with the need for more extended periods of time for the stories, he generally found a corner in the kibbutz library where he could work. It was of course out of the question that he be given any sort of dedicated workroom. And the writing had to be done at night because, like all the members of the kibbutz, he was putting in a full day of agricultural labor six days a week. A number of years down the road, when Amos's earliest publications sparked interest and admiration, even generating income, Hulda came by stages to accept his role as a writer. But it was not until 1975, when all the royalties from his books, as always going to the kibbutz, became quite substantial, that he was able to enjoy the convenience of a small room that served as a study.

In the early years of his marriage, before acquiring a study, he was constrained in another way to find a place to write. Like so many Israelis in that era, Amos was a chain-smoker, and he smoked constantly while he wrote. He couldn't do this at night in their bedroom because the smoke bothered Nily, so he went into the nook that housed the toilet and shut the door, put down the toilet seat, and, sitting on it, laid across his knees a large volume of Van Gogh reproductions that was a wedding gift and used that as a desk. The cramped quarters did not appear to have cramped his style. But the accumulation of smoke in that tiny enclosed space must have been chokingly dense.

Eventually, Amos would be given days off from his work obligations on the kibbutz to focus on his writing. He initially asked for one day a week. The request was granted rather grudgingly. As his royalties grew, all still going to the kibbutz, he was given three days and then finally five out of the six of the workweek. In this era, long before the movement of privatization that swept through most kibbutzim, no one had private money, so it was a matter of course that all the proceeds of Amos's publications would go directly into the kibbutz coffer. But as the proceeds increased, they were palpably enhancing the economy of the kibbutz, so Amos's productions came to be thought of as a "branch" (*anaf*) of the kibbutz enterprise, parallel to the branches of poultry, dairy production, and the sundry crops. When Amos left Hulda in 1986, the kibbutz refused to give him the customary substantial separation fund, arguing that he was taking away an appreciable source of revenue. He and Nily had to start a new life in the Negev town of Arad almost without financial resources.

The first piece of writing that Amos published during his early years at Hulda was not fiction, however, but an engagement in ideological debate, making it the harbinger of a significant type of writing that he would pursue to address the urgent questions of public policy and politics that pressed upon Israel. In January 1960, when Amos was not yet twenty-one, David Ben-Gurion, Israel's revered first prime minister, published a piece in *Davar*, the newspaper of the Labor party, in which he argued that the kibbutz movement, founded on the principle of equality, proceeded from an idea that had no anchorage in reality, and that the guiding principle of the kibbutz should instead be cooperative existence, which was more realistic and could actually be implemented. Amos formulated a lengthy rejoinder, also published in *Davar*. While taking pains to speak respectfully of Ben-Gurion, he proposed that an aspiration to attain the grand ideal of human equality, even if it could never be fully realized, was important to hold on to as a powerful animating force for the kibbutz movement. Ben-Gurion read this rejoinder and invited its young author to come see him in his office.

This episode is narrated in detail in *A Tale of Love and Darkness*, which does not, however, report the substance of the original article or the rejoinder. The meeting is conveyed in what amounts to high comedy, though in writing about it, Amos lets the comic aspect of the meeting speak for itself, merely describing what transpired in the encounter. Ben-Gurion greets the young kibbutznik warmly, then launches on a virtually uninterrupted monologue, at the end of which he tells Amos that it was a pleasure to have this conversation with him and that he hopes they will have the opportunity to speak again. With the passage of time, as Amos became a public figure, each of Israel's prime ministers, including right-wing leaders, would make some contact with him to discuss issues and perhaps even to take counsel with him, although it is unlikely that any of them followed his advice. In a manner hard to imagine in America, where writers have almost no presence in the political sphere, Amos Oz came to be regarded across much of the political spectrum as someone whose opinion perhaps should at least be heard. In any case, the published rejoinder to Ben-Gurion and the invitation to meet him were an early indication of the move Amos would make to the public stage.

A very different portentous experience overwhelmed Amos more than a year after his arrival at Hulda. Since crossing the threshold of puberty in Jerusalem, he had, like most young males, experienced a simmering soup of hormones that led to bouts of self-pleasuring. Although the way he writes about them suggests he didn't think of them exactly as sinful—after all, he had not been subjected to the post-Victorian instruction that masturbation is a moral transgression and a grave danger to the health of the body and the mind—he did feel there was something shameful about these impulses that he could not control. And though he had been a lovely-looking child and was certainly quite handsome as an adolescent, he suffered from the cultural prejudice prevalent far beyond Israel that encourages boys to think that physical attractiveness is a kind of female monopoly and that its feminine possessors are powerful and for the most part unattainable objects of desire. During his second year on the kibbutz, he was drawn to an object of desire that it would have seemed altogether unrealistic to attain.

At the age of sixteen, he had a teacher named Orna who was not a kibbutz member but had a home and a husband in Tel Aviv. She was thirty-five and had no children, though later she would have a daughter with her second husband. She read poetry and listened to classical music with Amos, whom she obviously recognized as a sensitive and gifted boy. One night he came to her room and, finding she was not there, sat on a mat and pulled back the curtain covering her clothes closet, where he saw displayed her colorful underwear and an almost transparent apricot-colored nightgown. He was powerfully aroused by the vision of these accoutrements of female allure. When Orna came back into her room and saw the insistent mound in his trousers, she drew close to him, gently reassuring, and began to undress. She showed him what to do, and he was overcome by the lightning-shock gratification of his first sexual consummation. After a brief while, they made love again. Orna then told him, still with reassuring gentleness, that they could not repeat this, that afterward their relationship had to be as it had been before. All this is narrated by Amos in his autobiographical book with great delicacy of feeling.

Now, there is a temptation to invoke as explanation some sort of vulgar Freudianism: four years previously he had lost his beloved mother, to whom he was oedipally attached, and now he fulfilled his sexual yearnings with a mother-figure. The notion may have an element of truth, but it is too simple, and his sexual behavior as an adult shows no evidence that he was driven by an oedipal fixation. The more crucial link for his consummation with Orna is to a prepubescent episode recorded in *A Tale of Love and Darkness* about his attachment to Teacher Zelda. He was ten and that attachment could not yet have been consciously sexual. In any case, Zelda, demure and modest in her ultra-Orthodox attire, would not readily have suggested herself to a prepubescent boy as an object of erotic desire. But the boy's infatuation with her was definitely romantic: he thought of her constantly, and when an appropriately adult Orthodox suitor, who in fact would become her husband, appeared on the scene, the boy was intensely jealous. His desire for Orna—in this case, clearly an erotic form of desire—replicated many of the components of his romantic longing for that highly idiosyncratic and charismatic teacher that he experienced at the age of ten. Orna, too, was his teacher and the kind of mentor who had identified him as a gifted boy, as Zelda had done, and taken him aside to guide him, as Zelda had also done, to discover new cultural riches. The age gap, moreover, between her and Amos is similar to that between the boy and Zelda, who was then around thirty: in both instances a twenty-year difference.

Amos concludes the Orna story with two brief paragraphs of rather startling reflection about how he has conceived his relation to women ever since. After that evening in Orna's room, he writes, "It still always seems to me that woman holds the keys to desire[. . . .] The favors women grant stir in me, besides arousal and amazement, a wave of childish gratitude together with an impulse to bow down to the woman: I am unworthy of all these wonders." My conclusion from this is not that Amos's sexual identity had anything stunted or otherwise wrong with it as he went on in life, but perhaps many men never entirely outgrow an adolescent vision of women and the fulfillment of desire. Amos ends this passage by articulating a fantasy about women and childbirth that is manifestly, even excessively, Freudian: "Why, when I came into the world, a woman awaited me at the entrance to whom I had just caused sharp pain, yet she granted me tender mercy, good recompensed for evil, and offered me the breast. The male, by contrast, lay in wait for me at the entryway with a circumcision knife in his hand."

Despite this talk of nurturing breasts and threatened castration, Amos began at Hulda to develop a relationship with a girl his age that was not in the least oedipal. The girl was Nily. Both she and Amos happened to be the children of librarians, but that was the only common thread between them: everything else was a study in contrasts. Those book-tending fathers themselves were opposites. Nily's father was unflaggingly cheerful, good-spirited, optimistic, and had a personality that appealed to all around him. Arieh Klausner was socially insecure, a compulsive talker, a pedant, and a man who nurtured fantasies about his own professional future that he would never be able to realize.

Amos and Nily became close friends but were not yet a couple when they left the kibbutz to do their army service. In fact, Amos took up with someone else at the age of sixteen, scant months after Orna introduced him to sex. Her name was Ilana, and they met on a ship sailing from Marseille to Haifa on his return voyage from a visit to his father in England—a visit, he felt, that had been a painful failure. They would remain a couple for four years, but in the latter part of this period, their relationship was shaken because Ilana had become involved with another man while still wanting to retain Amos as a boyfriend. Amos, unsurprisingly, would not agree to being second fiddle, so he broke with Ilana. To an impartial observer, she would seem to be the one at fault, but, curiously, toward the end of his life, when Amos told his friend Nurith Gertz about Ilana, he said he felt guilty for abandoning her. Having been abandoned by his mother through the traumatic event of her suicide, he was loath ever to abandon anyone, so even in this case, in which she had certainly triggered the abandonment by seeking to juggle two lovers, he was plagued with remorse. In the final weeks of his life, Nurith located Ilana for him. After a hiatus of more than sixty years, he phoned her. She was shocked to hear his voice, but she came to see him a few times, and she reported to Nurith that they both felt good about their reunion. The reunion amounted to a kind of restitution for his imagined betrayal of his first girlfriend when they were not yet twenty.

Nily, however, was the real lodestar of his romantic life. What drew them together? On her part, there was surely an element of compassion for the boy she rightly saw as a sad and lonely orphan, mocked and harassed by many of his peers on the kibbutz. She also sensed that he was an unusually sensitive and imaginative person. Her acceptance encouraged Amos to show her, cheerful as she was, the melancholy poems he was then writing, poems that would almost certainly have elicited derision from most others among the young kibbutzniks. His strikingly good looks must also have drawn her. Amos, on his side, was attracted to a pretty girl who in many ways was his polar opposite. In *A Tale of Love and Darkness*, he says: "Nily spread all around her a kind of prodigal *joie de vivre*, which spilled forth unrestrained, a joy without rhyme or reason, without basis, without motive. Nothing needed to happen in order to make her overflow with sheer exuberance." In the tribute to Nily that Amos delivered at a public celebration in Arad on the occasion of her sixtieth birthday, he says much the same thing, adding that he found Nily altogether radiant. "Nily was a kind of firefly, a perpetual and inexhaustible source of light."

As we can readily see, Nily figured in his imagination as the great avenue out of the enclosure and gloom of Kerem Avraham, out of the tiny basement apartment with its dim light bulb that scarcely dissipated the darkness and away from the stiffly well-meaning but never adequate father, away from the mother plunged in depression. On an expedition to Jerusalem not long after their early marriage, Amos took Nily to see "Mr. Agnon." The great novelist, then in his seventies, was gracious to the young couple, and he told Nily she bore a strong resemblance to Amos's mother—"may she rest in peace," he piously added. As far as I can tell from looking at photos of Fania Klausner and being quite familiar with Nily's appearance, the resemblance was fanciful, but it was also a high compliment, for Agnon remembered Amos's mother fondly as a beautiful woman who was always charming and refined. In point of fact, the radiant, optimistic, physically vibrant Nily was in almost all respects the very antithesis of Amos's mother. She gave Amos a delightful release from the claustral world of his childhood, in which his mother sat darkly frozen at the center.

In those four years with Ilana, Amos was not likely to have thought much about his kibbutz friend Nily; he imagined, perhaps with some basis in fact, that she was constantly surrounded by suitors. After high school, both went off to do their army service, three years for men, two for women. While Amos was in the army, he would regularly come back to Hulda for visits over Friday night and into Saturday. On one of these visits, early in 1960, when kibbutz members pushed back the tables in the dining room after the Friday evening meal and used the space for dancing, Amos stood watching Nily as she danced. She loved to dance, just as she flung herself enthusiastically into sports and hiking and music. All these were activities for which Amos felt himself ill-equipped. In fact, late in life, on a little slip of paper, he told Nily that the one thing he really wished he had done was learn to dance. On this particular evening, watching Nily dance mesmerized him: her movements on the improvised dance floor were the perfect embodiment of the *joie de vivre* he saw in her. After the Friday-night dancing, he approached her, told her she danced better than anybody else, and asked her what she was planning to do afterward. It turned out that she was on night-watch duty. He knew that at the end of the watch, it was the practice to prepare something to eat. At 2 a.m., he told her, I'm going to be very hungry. He was announcing that he would stay up to wait for her. Nily picked up the hint and brought him a hot meal at that hour. As they sat together, Amos took out from a photo album a picture of his high-school buddy, Reuven Rivlin, who one day would become the president of Israel. "He was a great dancer," Amos told her. He wanted to show her that he had a friend who was a real dancer, even if he was not.

The next morning they went for a walk in a wooded area of the kibbutz. In the happiness of that moment together, Amos said to Nily something she would never forget: "I would give a year of my life if it could be a Shabbat morning like this one now, but only that we would be married." Nily immediately realized that this amounted to a proposal of marriage and accepted on the spot. This must surely have been one of the shortest courtship periods on record, no more than nine or ten hours. The two had been like brother and sister in their high-school years, but now, after Amos saw Nily's magical dancing, they became a couple that would be together for the next sixty years. Early marriages are quite common in Israel. Still, Amos and Nily raced into this one, with the wedding taking place barely three months later, in April 1960. The bride and groom were not yet twenty-one. And with the family impulse that is so powerful in Israel, many young couples have their first child right away. Nily gave birth to Fania, pointedly named after the mother Amos had lost so early, a year later. This daughter would grow up to be extremely close to her father, and her presence in his life beginning when he was just twenty-one was a kind of restoration, a way of freeing him at least to a limited degree from the cloud of orphanhood that had clung to him. Through the long years of the marriage, Amos and Nily would remain very close. She read all the drafts of his writing, often expressing her keen approval, which meant much to him, occasionally offering an objection to a particular formulation, which he always took seriously. She accompanied him on many of his trips across the world, and they shared the pleasures of discovering new places, new sights, new cultures. Very early marriages often prove within a few years to be ill-considered, but not this one.

I have not yet touched on the nature of Amos's military service. For that, I will need to go back in time to three years before that pivotal Friday night at Hulda. Amos's entry into military service after high school was eased by his having been sent to Jerusalem for a year to be part of a program sponsored by the kibbutz movement for young people before their actual recruitment into the army. There he became a battalion head in a Scout unit. A few months into this position, he was visited by Nily and a few others from their kibbutz. She found him transformed. As the group leader, he was now self-assured, authoritative, embodying upbeat confidence. This was an important moment of transition for Amos. At Hulda, he had only partially emerged from his awkward role as bookish outsider. Now he was assuming responsible tasks in what all the young people in that era would have regarded as an important and vital undertaking in Israeli society. Amos Oz the poised social presence emerges at this point. We may speculate that Nily's new perception of Amos as a capable person who was not in any obviously visible way an orphan helped make her ready on that Friday night and Saturday morning at Hulda three years later to return Amos's love and immediately agree to marry him.

It is well to keep in mind the difference between Israel a decade after the founding of the State and the Israel of the twenty-first century. Amos did not have a militaristic bone in his body, but in a time when Israel was repeatedly threatened by *fedayeen*, armed Arab infiltrators, and by the armies of the surrounding

Arab nations, it would not have occurred to a young man to resist military service or to see it as anything but a compelling
national duty to be embraced wholeheartedly. But regardless
of Amos's willingness to serve, during his basic training his su-
periors quickly saw that he was not cut out for combat duty, so
they placed him in an education unit. When he was called up as
a reservist to serve in the wars of 1967 and 1973, it was his writing skills that the army made use of, these being deployed, however, on the front line.

In any case, the three years of compulsory military service
were uneventful. When Amos completed them, his kibbutz decided to send him to Jerusalem to earn a bachelor's degree, for
Hulda was in need of a high-school teacher, and the inveter-
ately intellectual Amos was obviously suited for the position.
Studying philosophy and literature, he managed to earn his degree in two years instead of the usual three. At the Hebrew
University, Amos took a philosophy course with Hugo Bergman,
Kafka's classmate from Prague, with whom Amos's mother had
studied in the late 1930s at the Hebrew University. It was a peculiar course. Bergman, at this point late in his career, sought to
persuade his students that the self persists after death, which we
know because none of the constituents of the universe entirely
disappears but is transformed. Bergman may have made some
impression on Amos as a charismatic—and historical—presence,
but his eccentric views on immortality had no impact, as we can
see from Amos's unblinking reflections on death in a late volume of taped conversations. Another professor of philosophy,
one whom Amos remembered with enthusiasm, was Nathan
Rotenstreich, then an intellectual eminence at the university. In
the field of Hebrew literature, Amos studied with the prominent academic figures of the early 1960s—Simon Halkin, Dov
Sadan, Gershon Shaked—though he did not comment on any
impact their teaching might have had on him.

While he was at the university, he made a lifelong friend

who would significantly influence what he did when he was called up as a reservist in 1967 and 1973. Yisrael Tal, fifteen years older than Amos, had been virtually baptized by fire. In the Arab attacks on the Jewish population of Palestine in 1929, when Tal was five, he and his mother and sister were trapped in their house in the town of Mahanaim. The house was set on fire, but the Tal family managed to escape. Tal joined the Haganah, the self-defense organization of mainline Zionism before the founding of the State, and then served in the Palmach, Israel's commando force, during the 1948–1949 war. He continued in the army, rising through the ranks in the armored corps. But in 1961, when he was passed over for the position of commander of the armored corps, he took time off from the army to acquire a degree in philosophy and social science at the Hebrew University. It was in a philosophy class that he and Amos met. Despite the age difference and the disparity in capabilities, the two established a deep rapport, and they would continue to remain close. Tal the career soldier must have had some intellectual inclinations, as his decision to study philosophy may suggest; later, when he retired from the military, he did a teaching stint at Tel Aviv University. So the seasoned warrior and the very bright young kibbutznik dedicated to literature found a common language. Tal returned to the military after completing his studies, fairly soon obtaining the position of armored corps commander that he had missed out on in 1961. He was promoted to the rank of general and played a key role in both the Six-Day War and the Yom Kippur War, by, among other things, identifying the need for improved firepower as crucial for the effectiveness of the tanks and armored vehicles.

When Amos was called up in 1967 and placed, according to his previous background in the army, in an education unit, Yisrael Tal got in touch with him and told him he needed his services for the armored corps, not to be a combatant but to formulate daily directives to issue to the forces. Tal was, in other words, asking him to bring to bear in the military his adeptness as a writer. Nily Oz, in the lengthy transcript of a set of oral reminiscences to a family member about her husband made at the end of 2019, not long after his death, and later published in Hebrew as a book, cites the text of one of Amos's directives, which is manifestly cast in language armies are unaccustomed to hear.

June 5, 1967
To the soldiers of the armored division:

The signal has been given!

Today we will go forth to smash the hand that has reached out to strangle us.

Today we will go forth to open wide the southern gate that was shuttered by the Egyptian aggressor.

Our armored force will carry the war deep into enemy soil. We took no joy in the battle. The enemy wanted it. The enemy launched it. And the enemy will get it back twofold.

Let us remember:

This is the third time the Egyptian dagger has been wielded against us. This is the third time the enemy was mistaken in the mad illusion: to see Israel on its knees.

In blood and fire we will tear this scheme out of his heart.

Let us also remember:

We are not at war with the citizens of Egypt. We do not seek to take their land and their property. We have not come to destroy their country or to seize possession of it.

- We boldly advance in order to crush the concentration of power that was meant to threaten our safety.
- We boldly advance in order to tear from their hinges the gates of the Egyptian blockade.
- We boldly advance in order to shatter the aim of destruction.

Today the Sinai Desert shall come to know the power of the armored division, and the earth shall tremble beneath it.

Presumably, this is a directive to the troops to attack the Egyptian forces.

Let us recall the strategic circumstances: Egypt had closed the Straits of Tiran to Israeli ships, thus cutting off Israel's connection by sea to India and the east. A blockade is considered an act of war in international law, and in June 1967, Israel acted on that premise. But virtually the only element of the quoted directive that is couched in factual terms is the opening, "The signal has been given," and even those words are heightened by an exclamation point. Everything else is rendered metaphorically, reinforced by the rhetorical device of emphatic repetition. The metaphors involved are ones that Amos Oz the novelist would blush to use, but their stereotypical character served the present purpose of rousing the troops to battle. Thus, the Egyptian blockade is a hand reached out to strangle. Nasser's massing of troops at the border is a dagger wielded against Israel. The Straits of Tiran are a shuttered gate to the south. In the sweep of these highly wrought words, Egypt is said to have threatened Israel three times—in 1948–1949, in 1956, and now—though in 1956 Israel was actually the aggressor. The traditional rhetorical terms of blood and fire and iron are reminiscent of the language Amos heard from the Herut stalwarts in his boyhood. A famous slogan of the Right was "In blood and fire Judea fell. In blood and fire shall Judea rise." This oration in the guise of a military directive concludes on a nearly biblical note: the Sinai Desert, which the Israeli force is about to invade, will "come to know" the power of this armored force, "and the earth shall tremble beneath it," a formulation that recalls evocations of cataclysmic destruction by the biblical prophets.

We should not conclude from this document that Amos Oz, even temporarily, had turned into a fiery nationalist. The hortatory rhetoric is framed to stir the fighting men as they are about to undertake an invasion. Not many days after formulating these words, when the smoke from the Six-Day War had barely cleared, he was arguing passionately that holding on to the Occupied Territories was a grave error, a position that he clung to till the end of his life. And while still on the Suez front, after hostilities had come to an end, he engaged in some minor negotiations about the separation of the forces with an Egyptian communications officer who spoke Hebrew. The two struck up a friendly relationship, met several times, and debated who could produce the best baked goods, the ones Nily prepared for Amos or those that the Egyptian's mother made for him.

Although Amos, prudently directed away from combat duty by his friend, was not wielding weapons, he was a close witness, as he would again be in 1973, to the havoc wreaked on the battlefield—the burned-out military vehicles, the mangled and charred bodies strewn all around, which at the Sinai front belonged for the most part to Egyptians but certainly included many fallen Israelis as well. Amos was loath either to speak or to write about what he experienced on the front lines, nor is his experience reflected in his fiction: there is no equivalent in his novels of David Grossman's searing representation in *To the End of the Land* of the Sinai front in 1973 during those early days of chaos. Amos was clearly disinclined to act as a chronicler of war. Perhaps an impulse somehow related to his long silence about his mother's suicide made him recoil from writing about things that were horrifying to him. Other Israeli writers were surely scarred by what they experienced on the battlefield, but Amos seems to have had a temperamental disinclination to confront horrors in his writing. In one late interview, however, he was asked directly what it was like in those two wars. His brief response, which he came back to in conversations with his editor Shira Hadad late in life, is startling: the main thing that hits you on the battlefield, he said, is the smells—the acrid smells of burning vehicles, the smells of exploded munitions, and, above all, the smell of rotting flesh.

Here he recounts an altogether visceral experience of the

consequences of armed combat. After the 1973 war, he told
Nurith Gertz, at their first meeting, which would begin a lifelong friendship, referring to someone who had been hit with a
round of bullets in the chest, "The last word that still lingers
before the scream is *Imma* [Mama] . . . I know this because I
was there, I saw it. He screamed '*Imma*.'" Amos would surely
have become a champion of the cause of peace in any case—he
was a leading figure in the Peace Now movement in Israel from
its beginnings—but experiencing the ghastly concrete meaning
of war through all his senses, and the olfactory sense in particular, may well have lent urgency to his repeated argument that
some way must be found to resolve the conflict between Israel
and the Palestinians other than through the force of arms.

In 1976, Amos had a near-death experience of his own in
the midst of which battlefield memories floated up. While he
was driving with his family, his car crashed, flipping over. His
daughter Fania, thirteen at the time, was unhurt, as was her
mother; his daughter Galia, four years younger, suffered minor
injuries. Their father, however, was gravely injured and had to
be rushed to a hospital in Jerusalem. He would remain there
almost half a year, much of the time in intensive care, his head
immobilized, both legs in casts, his breathing labored. As he
was taken on a gurney to the operating theater, anesthetized
and barely conscious, he managed to say, indistinctly, something
about Syrian tanks on all sides, a vast number of tanks, all headed
toward him. His two wars, the second on the Syrian front, had
left deep scars in his memory. We can understand why he decided not to write about it.

Amos's time in uniform, both during his compulsory service and in his two much shorter stints on the front as a reservist, did not allow him the leisure to pursue his writing goals.
Still, his drive to write remained a compelling force in these
years after his army service and quite soon after his marriage.
As he reports in *A Tale of Love and Darkness*, during his period

of acclimation at Hulda, he had found a key that opened the gates to writing fiction. In his adolescent struggles with the craft, he had imagined that great fiction had to be situated out in the broad world where important things were happening—in London, Paris, New York, Vienna. Then he discovered a Hebrew translation of Sherwood Anderson's 1919 volume of interlinked stories, *Winesburg, Ohio*. The book's subtitle—*A Group of Tales of Ohio Small-Town Life*—suggests precisely how it could speak to the young Israeli writer. Here was fiction, realized with accomplished artistry, that could be generally illuminating, even though it was tracking the life experiences of ordinary people located in a patently provincial setting, far from the major centers of the cultural, political, and social world. In a moment of revelation, Amos realized that the same could be done with the Israelis he knew in their own provincial world. So he began to write stories about ordinary people on a kibbutz.

This set the pattern for virtually all his future stories and novels. He was never tempted to move his fiction to the broad reaches of Europe or the Americas. As a Hebrew writer, he remained resolutely Israeli. But even while he dealt with issues specific to Israel—the sense of living in a state of siege, the troubled relationship between Israelis and Palestinians, the tensions of collective life on the kibbutz, the moral ambiguities of Jewish existence under British rule during the period of the Mandate—the characters and the dilemmas with which they struggle resonated with readers in far-flung places, their very different experiences notwithstanding. A general rule of good fiction may be that the more particular the writing, the more universal it is, at least if the writing delves deeply and unflinchingly into the particular. Nothing compromises fiction more gravely than the willed effort to make it universal. Amos Oz's stories and novels would be translated into many different languages, enjoying an international dissemination equaled among works by Israeli writers only by those of the great Hebrew poet

Yehuda Amichai. Amos's understanding of what *Winesburg, Ohio* meant had not been wrong. What he uncovered in his stories about the sequestered provincial lives of the kibbutzniks was not quite what might have been expected, for it had a certain connection with the darkness he continued to carry within him. Through these stories he would make his sudden leap onto the literary stage.

Amos's location on a kibbutz during the first half of his career was unusual for his generation of Hebrew writers. In the previous generation, when the kibbutz was more central to life in the Zionist community, a number of prominent writers were kibbutzniks. By the 1960s, the base of Hebrew literature had become preponderantly urban, so Amos, driving his tractor, taking his meals in the dining hall, removed from the bustling cafés of Tel Aviv, was an outlier. In contemplating the enclosed community around him through his fiction, he was able to turn it into a kind of laboratory for exploring the multiple ambiguities and frequent deviousness of human nature. I would also suggest that his relative isolation on the kibbutz encouraged him to follow his own path as a writer, relatively free from passing literary fashions and the cliques and warring factions of the urban literary world. No one else was writing the way he was, certainly in regard to style but in other ways as well. This flagrant differentness invited some sharp attacks by critics, even early on but especially later in his career. Nevertheless, the stories of his debut volume, perceived as something strikingly new in Hebrew fiction, also elicited considerable excitement, catapulting him to unusual prominence when he was barely twenty-six.

3

The Fiction Writer

AMOS BEGAN WRITING for publication very early. He had, after all, announced himself as an author as soon as he was able to pick out the appropriate letters on his father's typewriter, and by the age of ten he was showing his poems to Teacher Zelda. The writing of poetry continued during his first years on the kibbutz. Although he would discover by the age of twenty that what he really was cut out to write was fiction, an undertaking to which he then permanently dedicated himself, vestiges of the aspiring poet are detectable in his prose; later in his career he even wrote a novel in verse, *The Same Sea*. His first book of fiction, *Where the Jackals Howl*—the Hebrew title, *Lands of the Jackal*, more aptly emphasizes the geographical setting—appeared in 1965, when he was just twenty-six, and several of the stories were written two years earlier. The collection of stories follows the enabling model he had discovered in *Winesburg, Ohio:* the stories are focused, with one exception, on ordinary lives in a provincial place, the kibbutz, though the characters are not interlinked, as in Sherwood Anderson's work. The stories are not at all what would have been expected from someone ardently committed to the ideal of kibbutz life, and they reflect a good deal of the young Amos's deep inward brooding about the world, as well as his observations of the people around him.

Despite Amos's youth and his still being a relatively unknown writer, he had no difficulty securing a publisher for his first book. A few of the stories had initially appeared in prestigious literary journals, which would have helped. The main reason that the book was readily accepted, however, was that on its submission, the editors saw it as a strong and innovative development in Hebrew fiction. As his career went on, he never encountered problems placing his work with publishers.

When the book appeared, the Israeli literary establishment immediately recognized that Amos offered a new, altogether distinctive, voice in Hebrew fiction, and it embraced him, both in reviews and through public events. An evening devoted to *Where the Jackals Howl* was held at the Tzavta Club in Tel Aviv, the country's premier venue for literary events, in a gesture quite rare for debut books. Amos's fiction would quickly develop an enthusiastic following in Israel, and many of his books became bestsellers there.

Yet the approbation was far from universal. From early on, there were critics, and also some fellow novelists, who were put off by his writing, finding it extravagantly literary, high-pitched, given to excess. In 1968, Baruch Kurzweil, one of the country's most influential critics, published a withering attack on Amos's second novel, *My Michael*. Dan Miron, a central and prolific critic in the generation after Kurzweil, wrote caustically of Amos's fiction early and late and did not hesitate to mount a last attack immediately after the writer's death. At his best, Miron has been an astute and very learned critic. Over the years he has also become well known for savaging writers he doesn't like, probably a temperamental inclination. In the case of Amos Oz, he was put off from the beginning by what he called the "operatic" cast of the writing. Let me cite a few lines in a passage quoted earlier from *A Tale of Love and Darkness* in which Amos evokes the allure of death for his mother: "this vampire-suitor whose voice is bittersweet like the muffled sound of a cello on lonely nights, a velvet, subtle schemer, artist of plots, magic flutist who draws into the folds of his silken robe the lonely and the despairing." This is precisely the kind of prose that set Miron's teeth on edge, provoking him to sharp attack. I would contend that the extraordinary lyric fullness of the language aptly conveys the writer's sense of death as a powerful seduction for his suffering mother.

In due course, hostility from some quarters was probably exacerbated by Amos's great success as time went on and his work underwent multiple translations: there had to be something fundamentally suspect, according to a certain Israeli mentality, about a writer who sold books to millions of readers abroad. To a certain extent, Amos took note of these criticisms of his style, and as he went on in his career, he made an effort to lower the decibel level of his prose. This strategy was not, however, altogether congenial for him, inclined as he was to tap the multilayered riches of the Hebrew language, to write what is called an *Ivrit shel Shabbat*, which is to say, in a parallel American idiom, "Hebrew in its Sunday best." (This is evident in the lines just quoted from *A Tale*, a book that came relatively late in his career.) Moreover, his youthful impulse to write poetry was to a degree transposed into the prose of his fiction, sometimes with striking effectiveness, sometimes to the detriment of the prose.

In any case, the unusual success of this first book of stories inaugurated Amos's personal connection with people on the Israeli literary scene. One significant friendship was with A. B. Yehoshua, by most accounts the other most prominent figure in this new generation of writers succeeding those who had come of age around the time of the founding of the State. Although

a story circulated that Yehoshua and Amos had met when Yehoshua, three years Amos's elder, was his leader in a Scout group,
this was not the case. It was the publication of *Where the Jackals
Howl* that introduced Amos personally to his contemporary,
with whom he would remain close till his death. Yehoshua's
early stories reflected the influence of Kafka and of the surreal-
ist vein in Agnon. Stylistically, he was the antithesis of Amos,
deploying a terse, understated prose that was generally dead-
pan in tone. The two writers, having become devoted friends,
would see each other frequently, though there was, inevitably,
an element of rivalry in their relationship. Was there ever an
element of jealousy in their relationship? Perhaps. Be that as it
may, the strong bond between them stood the test of the years.
Yehoshua would express moving praise of his friend after he
died. Amos was not tempted to fling himself headlong into the
literary life of Tel Aviv, although the city was no more than a
short drive from Hulda. Instead, writers and critics often came
to the kibbutz to spend time with him.

What was new about *Where the Jackals Howl*, and what does
it tell us about the path that Amos was making for himself as a
writer at this early age? Also, what might it suggest about what
was going on with him as a person? The first thing readers in
1965 would have noticed was that the stories were cast in a kind
of Hebrew that was quite different from what they were accus-
tomed to finding in fiction. The previous generation of Israeli
writers, the first in which the novelists were native speakers of
the language, often made self-conscious attempts to emulate or
at least incorporate elements of the new spoken Hebrew. Amos
moved in the opposite direction. He notes in *A Tale of Love and
Darkness* how, as a child, he was enchanted by the magic of the
distinctly unmodern Hebrew he learned from Teacher Zelda,
a feeling later reinforced when he was exposed to a range of
traditional Hebrew texts in the Orthodox school to which his
parents decided to send him. With all these components of the

language fermenting in his imagination, he resolved to make
his own prose stamped through and through with many of the
resonances of the older strata of Hebrew even as its matrix
remained clearly modern. (In this last respect, he deliberately
swerved from the mesmerizing model of Agnon's prose, which
pervasively evoked the language of the early rabbis.) Amos
exercised an almost preternatural adeptness with the Hebrew
language. In time, his command of English would be quite impressive, too, but it did not approach what he could do with his
native tongue. Sometimes in his writing—certainly in this first
volume—his facility with the language could be dangerously
seductive to him as a writer, drawing him into sheer displays of
stylistic fireworks. Though his Hebrew in these stories cannot
be called archaizing, as Zelda's pupil, he fairly often substitutes
for a current term or idiom a locution taken from the anteced-
ent world of Hebrew texts, and this substitution sometimes even
infiltrates the dialogues in this collection.

Adjectives play an especially prominent role in this style,
and for a reason: the stories are repeatedly fashioned to convey
the feel of things—of the light at a particular moment of day,
of the shadows cast by a hill, of the sway of branches—and how
that feel of the surroundings impinges on the human actors,
invades them, shapes their world. One insistently reiterated syntactic pattern here is to front-load sentences with adjectives expressing the impact of the circumambient reality on those who
inhabit it. Thus: "Damp and torrid and enigmatic the evening
descended and its heat bit into the flesh like glass splinters." Or
again: "Gentle and calm was the dawn as it opened its eyes."
This adjectival freight is palpable as early as the first substantial
paragraph of the book:

> Finally the heat-wave relented.
>   A burst of sea-wind penetrated the hard frost of the
> dense torrid air and split chill cracks into it. First came hesi-

tant, light gusts, and the tops of the cypresses trembled in yearning as though a vital stream had gone through them, ascending from their roots and shaking their spine and permeating them with a wordless pampering.

Coupled with the prominence of adjectives is the transmogrification of what is ostensibly a report—in this instance, of weather and temperature as evening falls—into a portentously anthropomorphic description: the treetops tremble in yearning, the trees themselves have a "spine" (*shidrah*), and they are pervaded by a virtually erotic "pampering" (or "delight," *tafnukim*).

This imagining of the natural world as the arena in which compelling anthropomorphic events take place, driving or mirroring the human scenes of the stories, is ubiquitous in *Where the Jackals Howl*. Let me offer one further example among many:

> A purple radiance was kindled in the eastern mountains and the gentle wind joyously inflamed it. The sunbeams breaking through, powerfully and sharply, invaded the mountain of clouds. Dark cracks opened themselves to the burning heat and let the shards of brilliance sport with them. Finally, the torrid globe had second thoughts, flung itself against the wall of clouds, and pierced the eastern horizon. The delicate purple surrendered and gave way to a gleaming and terrible crimson.

This is more than a description of changing colors and clouds at sunrise. The sky and the clouds and the mountains on the horizon are suffused with tension and intimations of conflict: the rising sun flings itself against the wall of clouds, the crepuscular purple "surrenders" to a crimson that is "gleaming and terrible." We witness here the lyric gift of a writer who first aspired to become a poet. Through all this, with the dense representation of warring forces in the colors of the sunrise, the erstwhile poet is introducing a story, "The Way of the Wind," in which a parachutist will die falling out of the sky.

Where the Jackals Howl is manifestly the work of a rather

young writer. Some of the prose, powerful as it may be, seems overwrought, and at least a few of the symbolic correspondences seem excessively insistent, like the sexually frustrated woman in one of the stories who undergoes a rapturous *Liebestod* when she is fatally bitten by a venomous viper. In trying to follow where Amos Oz had come in his life by the early 1960s, the essential question is what this initial volume of stories tells us about his inner world. Rereading the book after the passage of more than half a century, I am struck by how dark the stories are. Death is a palpable presence in many of the stories. I have just alluded in passing to a woman erotically giving herself to death by snake-bite and a young man dying in a failed parachute jump, to which we can add a suicide and a young soldier lying dead in the field where his body is devoured by jackals. The kibbutz itself, a place ostensibly devoted to communal values and workers' solidarity, is peopled by sad, lonely isolates, many with repressed desires. Whatever sexual couplings take place among them seem brief and joyless.

And there are the jackals outside the kibbutz. Several critics, including me in an article I wrote back in 1969, have noted that the jackals beyond the perimeters of the kibbutz themselves constitute a primary image of the ontology that Amos Oz constructs in his fiction. This world-picture is worth reviewing here, for it recurs in different guises in much of his fiction. Inside the fences that surround the kibbutz is a planned community built on the idea that it is possible to impose rational order and light on human existence. Outside, in the dark and the wild, lurk menacing presences that threaten to destroy that possibility. A passage in the title story defines this opposition with singular clarity.

> In this twilight hour our world is circles within circles. The outermost is the circle of abstract, distant darkness: a murky lake swarming with agitations and murmurings.

Surrounded and shut down within are the nocturnal lands sprinkled with vineyards and orchards. Our lands betray us in the hours of the night. They are no longer reliable and submissive and known. Now our hard-won fields join forces with the kingdoms of the foe; like a silent and murky threat, they send out against us obscure, alien waves. Before our very eyes they bristle with an essence that is clotted, dark, hostile, and evil.

The circle of lights is what protects our little houses. This wall is exposed to the odors and the sounds of the foe that wail and revel.

The "foe"—not the usual Hebrew term for "enemy" but a word that also means "hater"—is extravagantly personified in these stories: "Suddenly, with dumbfounding speed, you are surrounded by them, besieged and petrified. Their eyes burn with everlasting hatred." It is altogether too easy to identify the hostile jackals of the description with a symbolic referent, the most obvious being the Arab forces holding Israel in a state of siege, the *fedayeen* being their infiltrator surrogates. But we are warned against such neat identifications when a character in one of the stories ponders the meaning of the jackals, which can be mistaken by identifying their "actual cry," which "is a known symbol of the destruction of kingdoms and of the madness and death that lie in wait for man. But these voices are stronger than the referents, sweeping them away, pouncing on the nakedness of man." The point is that the cry of the jackals conjures up a few overlapping yet different things, not all of them surfacing in consciousness: perhaps, indeed, these wild creatures are the actual human enemy; perhaps they are the menacing chaos of nature itself unsubdued by humankind; very likely, they are the dark destructive urgings within the individual psyche and in the human collective order. Here is a vivid illustration of how Amos Oz's very Israeli, localized fiction has a universal reach, for the encirclement of the kibbutz by the howling, hostile jackals becomes also a haunting picture of civilization and its discontents.

All this menace and death runs starkly counter to the life Amos was trying to live outside his writing and to the beliefs that he quite sincerely held. He was in the early years of a happy marriage to a buoyantly cheerful woman and the father of two daughters to whom he was devoted. At first perceived as an outsider by many of the kibbutzniks, he was now finally accepted in the Hulda community. And his adherence to the kibbutz ideal of creating a more equitable social realm than could ever be realized in capitalist society remained unflagging. What seems to be at work is the split I mentioned before between a reasonable, well-adjusted, flourishing self and a subterranean consciousness, the somber broodings of the boy orphaned at twelve whose wounds had never really healed. But this underground self was also why he had struck a new note in Hebrew fiction that many readers found arresting.

The Hebrew novels of the previous generation had been by and large socially oriented. Groups are often prominent in them—above all, the army, but also the kibbutz, which is very differently conceived from the way it is in Amos's fiction. The dilemmas facing the characters in the earlier novels are what can be called public dilemmas: How is a young soldier to think about his relation to the State and to his peers when he may be called on to sacrifice his life? How is a person to define an individual self and yet find ways to be integrated in a communal society? Against this background, Amos's fiction—and what was emerging in the writing of several others in his generation—was devised to draw readers into the inward recesses of the characters, to reckon with their erotic or violent or self-destructive impulses, the unconscious forces threatening the stability of individual agents, stability that had been broadly assumed in the Zionist enterprise.

To consider here in detail each of Amos's works of fiction is neither necessary nor feasible. I have lingered over *Where the Jackals Howl* because it establishes some of the characteristics of his writing as he goes on in his career. I will focus on his second novel, *My Michael,* because that is the book in which he attains full distinctive artistic maturity as a writer. Although I touch on other works, I will give special attention to the novella *Crusade* because even in being an anomaly in his writing, it touches on the matrix of his imaginative world and, indeed, of his psyche. Finally, I look in detail at his last novel, *Judas,* published four years before his death; it gives no sign that his powers are waning but instead shows his bold originality as an explorer of ideology through the medium of fiction.

As Amos was making his literary debut with the publication of *Where the Jackals Howl,* he was hard at work on his first novel, *Elsewhere, Perhaps,* which appeared the following year. Focusing on the intertwined lives in a fictitious kibbutz prudently located near Israel's northern border, far from Hulda, it again portrays a purportedly egalitarian society that is fissured by rivalries, envy, enmity, and wayward lust. Amos Oz, who had overnight become a known figure in Israeli culture, was in full momentum as a writer, and the pace would not slacken till near the end. Two years after the appearance of *Elsewhere, Perhaps,* he published his breakthrough novel, *My Michael* (1968). Over the next five decades, he would produce a dozen novels as well as several volumes of short stories and novellas and three books of fiction directed to younger readers, these last also of interest to adults and by no means to be excluded from his enterprise as a serious writer. His last novel, *Judas,* appeared in 2014, just before he was weakened by disease, but even after that, while depleted by the cancer that would prove fatal, he continued to turn out books: a consideration of political fanaticism, which he had had occasion to view close up beginning in his Jerusalem childhood, and then, in his last year and a half, his energy now waning, a series of taped conversations with Shira Hadad, his editor for *Judas*—a genuine friendship had emerged from their professional relationship. In the conversations he reflected on the vocation of literature, on writers and their readers, on his career as a writer, on sex, on women, on living and dying. All his writings and his expressed thoughts on writing constitute an avalanche of crafted words, including the recorded ones, from 1965 to 2018.

Let us now turn to *My Michael*, the book in which Amos hit full stride as a novelist and which also established his international reputation. When it first appeared, a good many Israeli readers were aware that the married couple depicted, Michael and Hannah Gonen, bore a distinct resemblance to Arieh and Fania Klausner in several respects. That resemblance needs to be examined because it shows how the writer's own life experience is both replicated and transmuted in the alembic of the fictional imagination. The broad outlines of connection are quite clear. The fictional husband, like Amos's father, is a rational, methodical man dedicated to systematic academic research—in his case, to achieving an advanced degree in geology, which will take him a decade to complete. There are few indications in his character of imagination, emotional expressiveness, or self-knowledge. His constantly tight self-control, always reflecting the same unexpressive reasonableness, at some points drives Hannah to distraction: "When will this man ever let loose. Just once to see him dismayed. Exulting. Wild." The fictional wife, like Amos's mother, studied literature as a university student and is literary even in her prolific fantasies; she is intensely emotional, fragile in health, and quite unstable. Her husband is considerate of her, as Amos's father was of his wife, but he never really understands her. At one point, as they lie in bed, after he has told her that he wonders whether she has stopped loving him, she thinks, "You are a stranger, Michael; you lie alongside me through the nights and you are a stranger."

A central technical move in *My Michael* bears some reflection. Amos decided to use Hannah as the first-person narrator of the book, not an easy thing for a male novelist to do with a female protagonist. Making her voice the voice of the story enabled him to jettison the sometimes excessively mannered style that had marked his debut as a writer. Since Hannah is always the one speaking, her narrative has a certain colloquial style, though her repeated flights of fantasy, often hallucinatory, are richly colored in a way that goes far beyond the colloquial. The reason for Amos's choice of Hannah as the narrator of his novel was both artistic and autobiographical. It was surely a way for him to penetrate the inner world of the mother who had ended her life so early, the mother to whom he had been much closer than he ever was to his father and with whom in some crucial ways he profoundly identified. All this enabled him to create a compelling voice for Hannah Gonen and to make this troubled young woman one of the remarkable female characters in fiction written in the second half of the twentieth century.

There is no simple equation between Hannah and Fania. Hannah does not become a suicide, though she certainly thinks a good deal about death in her dark musings. She also is repeatedly drawn to thoughts about sex, some of them quite violent, some masochistic, some relishing destruction as a kind of erotic fulfillment. She even goes through a brief phase in which she is impelled to make love to Michael with a fierce aggressiveness that startles and frightens him. This violently erotic aspect of Hannah is quite unlike any evident characteristic of Amos's mother. Whatever unknowable fantasies Fania may have harbored, her own shaky emotional life was expressed in a progressive retreat inward that terminated in the virtually catatonic condition of her last four years. Children never know much about their parents' sexuality, but what the young Amos could see of her decline and of the growing chasm between his parents suggests that both the decline and the chasm led her to a retreat from sex, as he may have intuitively sensed, not to an obsession with it.

Hannah Gonen, then, is a fictional character with many entirely distinctive features as an imaginative construct, but Amos's
understanding and memory of his mother's character are nevertheless tapped into for her creation. The very first words of
the novel could as easily apply to Fania—whose loved ones had
been murdered wholesale by the Nazis and whose awareness
of that loss no doubt aggravated her depression—as they do to
the fictional character enunciating them: "I am writing because
the people I loved have already died. I write because when I was
a little girl I possessed a great deal of strength to love and now
my strength to love is going to die. I don't want to die." Like
Fania, Hannah is addicted to dreaming. After recovering from
a protracted illness, she feels exiled from the world of dreams
that she had inhabited while ill: "I had lost the magic alchemy,
my gift for commanding the dreams to continue carrying me
beyond the border of waking. To the point where now I feel a
taste of collapse in each waking." Hannah's bleak words near the
end of her narrative could, again, have been spoken by Fania: "I
was afraid to die young and I was afraid to die old."

We should remember that Amos at this point in his life, in
his late twenties, had never uttered a word about his mother's
suicide, not even to Nily, his wife. But imagining a transformed
version of his mother in Hannah Gonen made it possible for
him to express many of his feelings about his mother's sad life
and her tragic end. That act of potent empathy through fictional invention also enabled him to achieve new powers as a
novelist. With this transformation of memory into a novelistic
figure, the great project of spinning out arresting fiction lay
open before him for the next six decades.

Amos brooded over two constant concerns for most of his
life: his childhood, with the trauma of his mother's suicide constituting its grim center, and the unrelenting predicament of
his country, surrounded by forces bent on its destruction and,
after 1967, containing a population of Palestinians that none of

67

its political leaders knew how to cope with. The brilliant move he hit on in *My Michael*, and what made it so resonant, was to combine these two preoccupations. The most striking respect in which Hannah Gonen is not Fania Klausner is that she is a troubled woman who conjures up Israel in a state of siege and in a time of recurrent terrorism as a projection screen for the disturbing emotions churning within her. Growing up in Jerusalem during the pre-State period—she would have been born around 1930—she is roughly a decade older than her author. As a young girl, she used to play with Arab twins, Aziz and Halil, who lived in her neighborhood. (There were no Arab families in Kerem Avraham, the setting of Amos's childhood, but their placement in proximity to Hannah as a child is crucial for the development of the novel.) Aziz and Halil become the focus of Hannah's erotic fantasies, her insistent longing for some kind of extraordinary release and fulfillment in sex that is nothing like her stale marital couplings with Michael. The last contact with the twins she recalls was when she was twelve or perhaps a little older. We infer that they fled to the other side of the border after 1947. In her distinctly erotic musings about the twins, she sees them as beautiful, almost wordless creatures, a view she despairs of explaining to her husband: "Two brownish gray wolves. Two lithe figures with white teeth. Two dark wild men. Two pirates. What do you know, Michael?" She fantasizes that they are now terrorists. The fact that they are twins fits the implicitly orgiastic character of her sexual fantasies, for being together with them would make a threesome.

For her to see them as wolves points to a portentous parallel with *Where the Jackals Howl*. They, too, are menacing wild creatures lurking in the dark beyond the defended perimeters of the Zionist state. Their gleaming white teeth, which will be noted later in the novel, are another link with the sharp-toothed jackals in the early stories. The important difference from the evocation of the jackals is that for Hannah the menace is what makes them alluring, not unlike the way the viper in *Where the Jackals Howl* becomes a sexualized agent of death.

Her fantasies about the twins vacillate. In one fantasy, she is terrified as she finds herself in a filthy cellar with a twin crawling toward her, knife in hand. More often, she yearns for Aziz and Halil even as they come to destroy. In the novel's spectacular conclusion, she conjures up the twins in a fantasy that fuses terrorism and eros:

> And on the slopes beyond the skyline there will be figures on a run that is a caress filled with longing, [. . .] the twisting path. The sky pressing against the cliffside. The nostrils distended to take in air. Fingers probing the crevices. Yearning of the hidden crickets. The damp of the dew and the wind. And suddenly but not suddenly, thunder of the muffled blast of an explosion. A glare of light flashes on the western horizon. Tatters of low clouds roll down the hollows of the mountain.
>
> And the burst of bleeding laughter. Strong and sweeping and vibrating. A hasty locking of fingers. The shadow of a lone carob tree up on the crest. The gulch. A soot-smeared lamp. First words. A shout of joy. Slumber. The purple color of night. Over all the valleys, heavy dew. A star. Clusters of impenetrable mountains.
>
> A quiet wind touches the pine trees again and again. The horizon slowly pales. And over the great spaces a cold tranquility descends.

This concluding passage is a mesmerizing expression of Hannah Gonen's roiling inner state. The gliding movements of the twins, now terrorists, are both the stealthy motions of infiltrators about to attack and a sensual caress. The explosion they detonate is also an orgasm, and the cold tranquility that descends afterward in Hannah's final fantasy is the quieting of the senses after orgasmic release—and perhaps it is also death.

What does this world of gripping, shocking fantasy tell us about the path Amos Oz was now blazing for himself as a novelist? At the very time he was writing this, 1967–1968, in apparent contradiction, Amos as a public intellectual was launching what would be a lifelong argument for peaceful reconciliation with the Palestinians. He himself underlined this split in "Act and Books," a 1976 article in the kibbutz journal *Shdemot*. There is an unbridgeable chasm, he proposed, between the realm of acts, which requires practical decisions with the means of implementing policy, and the realm of literature, which offers ambiguities and perceptions about experience that are not generalizations. We must draw a clear line, he proposed, between the articulation of public policy and the inventions of fiction.

Hannah Gonen is herself a symptom of Israel's national malaise, which is caused by its constant uneasy confrontation with the Arabs. In her fantasies, the Arabs are the murky menacing Other, frightening and powerfully alluring. The novels Amos Oz was writing were, as I observed, antithetical to the fiction of the preceding generation of Hebrew novelists. Even as his books arrestingly probed individual character, they were an exploration of the dark underside of Israeli national consciousness. At the same time, as *My Michael* came to command widespread international attention in multiple translations, it could speak to other places and other peoples, for all countries have their troubled underside, almost all individuals have dark unacknowledged places within. This novel is a signal instance in which the local place and habitation of Israel becomes a universal place. Hannah's spectral Jerusalem—"a faraway city, even when you live in it," she thinks—with its walls and crooked alleys and the mountains around it waiting to pounce, is also the city of everywhere.

As a coda to tracking what in *My Michael* reflects Amos's life and what is fictional invention, I want to present one moment in Hannah's story that is a link with Amos rather than with his mother. Hannah had been studying Hebrew literature at the Hebrew University. In a notebook, she wrote down something her professor had said in class, that there was a pervasive note of orphanhood in the work of Hebrew writers in Europe around the turn of the twentieth century. As a matter of literary history, this may or may not be accurate, but it certainly reflects the inner state of the novelist himself. Perhaps he also imagined Hannah Gonen as a kind of orphan, if not literally, then emotionally. She is terribly alone in the world, the figures of her fantasies her only true kin.

My Michael was Amos's breakthrough novel in two senses: because in it he found a way to flesh out a new order of penetrating psychological characterization and because it was the novel that established him as a widely read writer not only in Israel but internationally. The acclaim this book received through translations into many different languages had a significant effect on his life but not on his way of writing. Publishers in Europe and America were keenly interested in promoting the book, which for an author means appearances to do readings and talks before audiences both in large halls and in bookstores. Invitations also began to come for lectures and interviews beyond the initiative of publishers, and with the passage of time, these would multiply. Amos enjoyed the travels, on some of which he was accompanied by Nily, the two delighting together in the pleasures of new sights and new people. All this was very different from the life that could have been anticipated by a member of a small agricultural collective in the flatlands of Israel.

Amos and I first met on one of these early trips when in 1970 he came to the San Francisco Bay Area on a promotional tour. I did not hear his public presentation, but since he had read the piece on him and A. B. Yehoshua that I had published the previous year, he reached out to meet me. I remember taking him to dinner—it was just the two of us—at a Mexican restaurant in downtown Berkeley. This may have been his first encounter with Mexican food. When the waiter came to take our orders, I chose first and Amos said he would order exactly what I had. He was evidently on unfamiliar ground, perhaps a little cautious, but also curious to discover what there was to experience in this new place. I suspect that was his general disposition as he traveled from country to country.

Amos continued such journeys across the globe almost until the end, even when he was weakened by his terminal cancer. He was powerfully motivated to do this, not just because he wanted to promote sales of his books but, more importantly, because he came to love the interaction with audiences. He discovered early on that he had a special gift for engaging, even mesmerizing, audiences. I don't think, though, that it was because he relished having become a celebrity, however much he enjoyed the admiration. People who achieve some degree of fame but are not excessively egotistical are likely to sense something inauthentic in the adulation showered on them, to suspect that the expressed enthusiasm is for their public image, for what they have written or for what has been written about them, not for who they really are. That is the fate of the celebrity. Amos was not addicted to this sort of adulation, but he certainly experienced a deep sense of justifiable satisfaction in the magic he felt he could work when he laid out to audiences his ideas about political issues, about literature, and about his own books.

There was another reason why Amos did not become a total addict of celebrity. Much as he enjoyed his travels and his performances before audiences and the admiration he received, they never deflected him from what all along he felt was the overriding purpose of his life, which was to write. The frequent forays to foreign places were no more than temporary interruptions of his work as a writer, to which he always returned with a sense that this, after all, was the main thing he had to do. With the artistic confidence first realized in *My Michael*, Amos swung back and forth between the settings for his writings, between kib-butz and Jerusalem, often choosing for the latter the Mandatory period or the early years of the State when he grew up. Some-times he turned to other locations in Israel. Some of the books exhibited a hard-edged realism that was reflected in the language deployed. In others, or sometimes in passages in the more real-ist novels, he found ways to exercise the lyrical impulse that he always harbored, but now more artfully controlled, making it free of the stylistic mannerisms of his initial book of stories.

One novella written fairly early in his career, *Crusade* (1971)—the Hebrew title, *Unto Death*, more directly reflects the plot of the story—is an exception to the way he anchored his fiction in the Israeli scene and in the twentieth century. This hallucina-tory tale of a band of Crusaders making their way to the Holy Land, which they will never reach, dropping off one by one on their arduous and doomed trek, is Amos's meditation through fiction on the age-old Christian hatred of Jews. The prose is hauntingly lyrical, the perfect medium for depicting the crazed inner world of the Crusaders. Justifying that style, the novella is like a dream, one that is exalting for the dreamers but also mur-derous. It is a dream of a perfect Christian world, free of all men-acing aliens, and of Jerusalem as a shimmering city of redemp-tion where the Savior preached, was crucified, and rose to heaven, forever imparting a message of love to his believers. Amos Oz understood that dreams of perfection in our realm of imperfec-tion come to a lethal end: the dream of a pure race of Aryans led to millions of corpses; the dream of an ideal communist society led to the deaths of tens of millions of Russians and Chinese and to the killing fields of Cambodia. Such, on a small scale, its dynamics palpable, is the impelling dream of these Crusaders.

In his long career, Amos sometimes went back to the same settings and to similar themes, as in four different volumes fo-cusing on a kibbutz or an analogous small village, but he occasionally also undertook radical new departures. This foray into the Middle Ages and into the dark heart of European Christianity was unlike anything he wrote before or after, but it is unforgettable and expresses one of his abiding concerns.

The narrator offers many passages from the chronicle of one Crusader, Claude Crook-Shoulder. Here is one sentence of many that vividly evoke the collective paranoia compelling the group and eating away at it:

> There is an alien person in our midst. Night after night we all cry out in the name of the Savior but someone among us cries out a lie, and he is the Savior's enemy. A hidden hand once put out all the campfires in the third watch, and in the dark there was a scream in a language that is not a language of Christian folk. The Savior's enemy is hiding among us, a wolf in the midst of God's flock. The hand that put out all the campfires in the night is what brings death to our horses expiring in torment one after the other with an illness that has no like in the places where we dwell. When we approach the villages, the people there are warned in advance to conceal in the forest the food and the women and the horses. The Jews everywhere divine our coming, and the land that is a foe to us protects them.

The prose Amos fashioned for this grim subject avoids excess, even avoids melodrama, in dealing with a twisted collective consciousness. That effective artistic control continues to the very end of the novella, the eerie scene in which the last survivors of the band flounder through a snow-covered landscape that is far away from the Jerusalem of their fantasies:

> Not to their home to return. The countries of men have long been forgotten in their hearts. Nor to Jerusalem, which is perfect love and is not a place. They are more and more stripping away their bodies, more and more turning pure, into the heart of the glad song of the church bells and onward into the singing of the angels, leaving behind their despised flesh

and streaming inward, a white spurting over a white canvas,
an abstract intending, a melting vapor, perhaps rest.

Amos Oz was thirty-two years old when he fashioned these
words and this scene. Though he had written, and would write
again, about the daylit social world of the kibbutz, he was still,
as his wife saw him, the brooding orphan. There is surely an
imaginative echo here of the stories his mother told him as a
child, of dark forests where strange and menacing creatures
lurked. The doom-shadowed poetic quality of her sensibility is
given an expression in this novella that she could never have
achieved. Even more powerful in the shaping of his imagination is her early vanishing in a self-inflicted death. His mother's
presence and then her terrible absence at times drew Amos into
the murky underside of the human condition. His notion that
death for her, and implicitly for others as well, had been an alluring seducer is manifested in this historical fiction about the
obsessive hatred of the Jews. Here, at the very end of the novella, the Crusaders' relentless, ultimately suicidal drive to find
and destroy the sinister alien in their midst metamorphoses
into an embrace of death, a shedding of the burden of carnal
existence, an annihilation of materiality that could perhaps, at
long last for these tormented figures, bring rest. *Crusade* is a
remarkable imaginative achievement that is rooted in the dark
childhood memories of its author.

The surface world of Amos's writing is evoked through a
very different language from the one he uses for the interior
world of imagination, fear, fantasy. This other language tracks
the movement of the minds of the characters as they are engaged
in the social realm. It often is close to or actually is free indirect
discourse, which is to say, the unspoken words that the characters speak to themselves conveyed by the narrator in the third
person. Here, for example, is the opening passage of *A Perfect
Peace* (1982), arguably the strongest of Amos's volumes of fiction

about the kibbutz. In the brief initial paragraph, we are told that Yonatan Lifschitz, born and raised on the kibbutz that is the novel's setting, has resolved to leave his wife and the kibbutz and start a new life. These words record his initial train of thought:

> During his childhood, in his adolescence, during his army service, he was always surrounded in a close circle by men and women who never stopped interfering in his life. More and more he felt that these men and women were blocking something in him and that he should not continue to give in. They in the language they favored often spoke of positive developments or negative phenomena while he almost stopped understanding the meaning of the words. If he stood alone by the window at the end of the day and saw birds flying in the evening twilight, he would inwardly conclude that all of these birds in the end must die. If the announcer on the radio news spoke about the appearance of worrisome signs, Yonatan would whisper to himself, What difference does it make. And if he went out alone to wander in the afternoon by the burnt cypresses at the edge of the kibbutz and some kibbutznik ran into him and asked what he was doing here, Yonatan would answer listlessly: I'm just walking around a little. And his heart within would repeat the question, puzzled: What are you doing here. A good guy, they said about him on the kibbutz, but, you know—closed off, a sensitive type, they said.

We immediately see that, unlike in his earlier writing, there is absolutely no hint of excessive stylistic ornamentation here, no willed attempt to be literary. The words are the words such a person as Yonatan Lifschitz would have spoken to himself, and the words he hears from others on the kibbutz and on the radio news are the conventional formulas, respectively, for dutiful socialists and for news reporters—words that had come to be meaningless to him. This is a straightforward and convincing representation of a kibbutznik in the throes of an existential crisis, a man feeling he has lived all of his life responding as he was

expected to by others. He constantly feels the pressure of a conformity that he can no longer bear. All this surely expresses something of Amos's own sense of the tension between self and group,
initially in his Jerusalem childhood but especially on the kibbutz.

Some readers may wonder about this passage and the novel
as a whole that it introduces: How loyal could Amos Oz have
been to the kibbutz? Around forty when he began to write *A
Perfect Peace*, he had been part of Hulda for a quarter of a century, except during his three years of army service and his brief
time at the Hebrew University. This representation of a person
estranged by the obligations of collective living might lead to a
suspicion that Amos was in the kibbutz but inwardly alienated
from it, but that suspicion would be a mistake. The task of serious novelists is to depict the reality they know, warts and all.
The expression of political views and policy proposals is quite
another matter, as he himself noted in the short article "Act and
Books." In the novel, he can freely draw on the kinds of people
with whom he was familiar, "comrades" (*haverim*) in a manifestly imperfect society where socialist solidarity is often a dubious proposition and where many find that they are paying an
emotional price for collectivism. In this respect, *A Perfect Peace*
is continuous with the stories in *Where the Jackals Howl*; its characters are related to those desperate isolates that figure in the
stories. None of this puts into question Amos's unflagging loyalty to the idea of the kibbutz. What he proclaimed in his early
article responding to Ben-Gurion is a belief to which he continued to cling: the ideal of equality may be unrealizable in any
society, but it is worth adhering to as an enabling aspiration.

Loyalty notwithstanding, in 1986 Amos and Nily left Hulda
to take up residence in the Negev development town of Arad.
The reason for the move was medical. Their son, Daniel, then
eight, had been suffering from asthma attacks since infancy, and
his doctors proposed that he would do much better in the dry
desert air of the Negev. Daniel was born virtually a generation

after his two sisters, both at this point launched on their adult careers, Fania as a historian and Galia as an author of children's books. "We raised our own grandchild," Amos humorously remarked to me. Daniel would eventually move past this ailment and become a poet and a jazz musician.

In the spring of 1992, my wife and I went to Arad to see two of our three sons, Gaby and Dan, who were there for the year. Amos and Nily had been generously hospitable to them, and when we got in touch, they invited all of us to their apartment for a Saturday brunch. Amos had not visibly changed since I last saw him at Hulda, but Nily had: in the middle of the morning, she was wearing what looked to me like a black cocktail dress, and she was carefully made up and wearing high heels— the very antithesis of the kibbutznik in work clothes and demeanor whom I had seen at Hulda on some earlier occasions. Over brunch, I asked them what it was like to have left the kibbutz. Amos did not respond, but Nily, who had grown up at Hulda, told me that when you live on a kibbutz, you reflexively adopt the mental strategy of soldiers on the battlefield: what you see all around you is too horrific to bear, so you somehow create an inner distance from it, not quite seeing it even as you do. Perhaps this comparison was a little melodramatic, nor am I sure that Nily felt that way at all times. As for Amos, he may not have keenly missed Hulda nor have been nostalgic about it, but he did retain an abiding commitment in principle to the kibbutz ideal.

Arad was altogether different both from Hulda and from the Jerusalem of his childhood. The streets, at least then, were sand-strewn and a little bleak; the rows of shops, meager; and the surrounding desert could be seen and felt everywhere. Amos, however, in this second major displacement in his life, adapted, perhaps even eagerly, to the new location. He made friends among the locals, and he enjoyed the ethnic variety of the population. He also developed what can be called a special relationship with the desert. In several different televised interviews during his years in Arad, he offered an account of his writer's day. He would get up before dawn, dress, and go off for a walk by himself in the desert for an hour or more. We have to imagine the desert of Israel's Negev region not as a Sahara-like expanse of smooth sand but as rocky, with parched shrubs, perhaps a little like Death Valley, California. The emptiness and the bright light of the desert landscape were somehow bracing and clarifying for Amos. The vastness of the desert had the effect of putting his limited human life into perspective, leading him to look at his own existence under the aspect of eternity. Albert Camus, in a couple of the remarkable stories collected in *Exile and the Kingdom*, registers a similar response to the desert of his native Algeria. For Amos, the two previous settings of his life, the cramped quarters of both Kerem Avraham and Hulda, were in very different ways locations in which humanity crowded around him. He experienced the Negev desert, then, as liberating, or at least offering a liberation that was nourishing for him as a writer. In an interview with an ecological journal in 2012, when he had been in Arad more than two decades, he spelled out this feeling:

> The desert imposes a sense of quietude and tranquility on the things I write and on the rest of my doings [. . .]. The fact that I've begun the day in the midst of this great emptiness of the desert helps puts everything in proportion—what is enduring and what is ephemeral, what is serious and what is not.

After the desert walk, Amos would return to his apartment, usually by 6:30 a.m., have a quick breakfast, and sit down to write for the next few hours. The Arad years were not necessarily more productive for him—his drive to write meant that he was always productive—but they provided a comfortable regimen for him as a writer. And it is possible that the stillness of the empty landscape, after those decades of having people crowded around him, encouraged an impulse of unblinking retrospection. It was during the Arad years that he wrote the partly autobiographical *The Same Sea* and, soon after, *A Tale of Love and Darkness*.

The location in Arad brought with it a new professional engagement, one that was ancillary to Amos's work as a writer and personally congenial for him. Beginning in 1987, Amos occupied a position teaching literature at Ben-Gurion University in Beersheba, an easy commute from Arad. He had a flair for teaching and keenly enjoyed it. Two perceptive critical books emerged from his role as a professor, *The Silence of the Heavens* (1993), his study of Agnon's modernist masterpiece *Only Yesterday*, and *The Story Begins*, an account of strategies for beginning narratives. In the latter book we can see a direct move from the desk of the working writer to the lectern of the university professor. Amos continued at Ben-Gurion University until 2014, when he was well past the mandatory age for retirement in Israel. He and Nily then moved to Tel Aviv, the big city from which he had previously kept a distance; the move was mainly to be closer to their children and grandchildren.

One further aspect of Amos's personal experience fed into his writing. From his early exposure to right-wing Zionism and its fiery, uncompromising rhetoric, to which can be added the dogmatic socialism of some of his fellow kibbutz members, he had a vivid sense of how the passionate commitment to an ideology can shackle the mind and distort perception. One of the traits distinguishing him from other Israeli novelists was his ability to represent ideological intransigence, a feature of Zionist existence in his childhood years, as it still is in the present. This topic he dealt with in a whole series of novels and novellas. In his remarkable novella *The Hill of Evil Counsel* (1976), set in the late Mandatory years, a young man called Mitia, one character of several in this ideological mold, thunders denunciations of "perfidious Albion." His apocalyptic language is insistent even in a whisper to the father of the boy who (retrospectively) narrates the story. To the father Mitia says, "Jerusalem, which kills its prophets, will burn the modern Hellenizers in hellfire." "Hellenizers" is a reference to the Jews of Late Antique Palestine who embraced the ways of their Greek overlords and collaborated with them in the period of the Maccabean uprising. What such rhetoric implies is a typological view of history—the patterns of Late Antiquity are seen to manifest themselves again in modern times. As Amos understands, that is not a valid view of history. He himself was vulnerable to the mesmerizing magic of old Hebrew words, as he attests in *A Tale of Love and Darkness*, but he grasped how such words could steer someone into the abyss in the real political world.

Perhaps the most affecting representation of the crippling effect of fanaticism is in the novel for young readers—but definitely for older ones as well—*Panther in the Basement* (1995). This story, too, unfolds during the British Mandate. Its protagonist is a boy who would be about the same age that Amos was then and who similarly lives in Jerusalem. (In a late talk, he revealed that the plot was based on an experience he himself had as a child.) The book's protagonist, too, has been raised with the belligerent rhetoric of militant Zionism, chiefly directed against "perfidious Albion" at this moment in the 1940s. The boy, fearing the worst from a British sergeant who finds him roaming the streets after curfew, is befriended by him. The soldier, a religious Protestant, speaks to him in the biblical Hebrew he has learned, which produces some comic effects in the original. They agree to an uneasy pact in which the sergeant is to teach the boy English while learning modern Hebrew from him. The man's kindness and good intentions are clear, but the boy has a gnawing sense that he has been fraternizing with the enemy. The kids he hangs out with, militant Zionists like him and fancying themselves members of a combat unit of the resistance, like the Irgun, discover his relationship with the British sergeant and summon him to a kind of kangaroo court where they denounce him as a traitor. The ideology on which he has been nurtured tells him he must indeed be a traitor if he has consorted with a uniformed agent of his nation's sworn foe. His natural response as a boy to a very kind man tells him that no betrayal is involved. The conflict between an ideologically inculcated conscience and a spontaneous human response shapes a touching story that is virtually a parable about the moral dangers of a fanatic mind-set. For an American analogue, we might recall how Huck Finn is convinced he has done a terrible wrong in helping Jim escape from slavery; as readers, we recognize that he has done something humane for a man who becomes his friend.

Amos's last novel, *Judas* (2014), is worth some detailed attention because of what it says about his lifelong connection with politics and writing. Shortly after he finished writing it, he was diagnosed with the cancer that would prove to be terminal, but he was still impelled by the sense he had had since childhood that writing was what he was meant to do in this world: he would go on with it as long as he could. This novel shows no diminution in his creative powers. The prose throughout is strong and evocative. The setting of the novel—Jerusalem toward the end of the 1950s—is beautifully portrayed: the city, at once shabby and colorful, is represented during a long, cold, rainy winter under somber skies. Toward the end, we get the dawning of spring with its bright light and gentle air.

What strikes me as most riveting in this valedictory novel is the way it deals with ideological clashes, long a concern of the author's but taken up here in a bold new way. There are three interlocutors in the book, to which we may add a fourth, dead for several years at the time of the action but still a powerful presence. The protagonist, Shmuel Asch, is a dropout from a master's program at the Hebrew University who has taken a job as a companion for Gershom Wald, an aged invalid and nonstop talker in florid Hebrew studded with biblical quotations who needs someone to listen to his flood of talk several hours each day. There is one other resident in the house where Shmuel is given an attic room, a woman in her early forties named Atalia Abravanel. She is quite attractive (the writer repeatedly devotes attention to her carefully chosen clothes), sexually enticing to Shmuel but also sexually elusive, imperious, embittered, and emotionally enigmatic.

Through Atalia, the fourth interlocutor, now deceased, enters the novel, and he will prove to be the center of its foray into ideology. He is Atalia's father, She'altiel Abravanel (his first name is unusual; the last name is associated with a Sephardic aristocratic background). He had been an important member of the executive committee of the Jewish Agency, the government-in-waiting before the establishment of the State. As the debate at the United Nations over the fate of Palestine began, he turned out to be a Zionist who was nonetheless adamantly opposed to the creation of a Jewish state. A fluent speaker of Arabic with many Arab friends, he believed that the two peoples could co-exist in amity, that nations were a historical anachronism, and that the Zionist insistence on an independent state would lead only to endless bloodshed.

Abravanel's daughter had married Gershom Wald's son in 1947; a year later, the son was killed in action on the embattled road to Jerusalem, his body hideously mutilated by Arab fighters. Well before this, Abravanel had been forced to resign from the Zionist executive committee because of his heretical views. He was widely reviled as a traitor.

After the death of Wald's son, Wald was invited to live in Abravanel's home by the dissident, now a pariah withdrawn from the world. Abravanel's widowed daughter is the third person in the household. She carries forward her father's anti-statehood legacy after his death, voicing it perhaps even more vehemently than he would have done because of the dire fate of the husband to whom she was so briefly married. The permanent houseguest

Wald, on the other hand, is a mainline Zionist and a devoted follower of Ben-Gurion, a figure who had become anathema to She'altiel Abravanel.

In this complicated ideological scheme, the stigmatizing of Abravanel as a traitor is directly connected with the work Shmuel Asch had been doing as a graduate student. His ardently leftist politics—he pins pictures of Fidel Castro and Che Guevara on his wall—nevertheless allows him to remain within the Zionist consensus. His uncompleted research project, however, reflects an aberrant viewpoint on the founding story of Christianity. In it, he seeks to make the argument that Judas, vilified through the centuries as the arch traitor, was actually the most faithful of Jesus's followers. In Shmuel's version, it was Judas, fervently believing in Jesus's role as messiah, who persuaded the hesitant prophet from Nazareth to come to Jerusalem, provoke the authorities, and allow himself to be crucified, after which he would miraculously descend from the cross, manifesting his divine nature to all humankind. When the expected miracle failed to occur, Judas was driven to despair, and that is the reason he killed himself. Yet his misguided effort in a way enabled Jesus's mission, for, without the crucifixion, there would be no Christianity, no redemption through this sacrifice. Here the person called a traitor was the truly faithful one, a notion Amos invoked several times in his late public lectures, arguing that those who follow the dictates of their own conscience are likely to be denounced as traitors, an accusation in fact often directed at him by the Israeli Right.

At several points in the novel, the former graduate student is aghast at Atalia's angry expression of her father's anti-Zionism, but he finds himself unable to respond. Here is one of her characteristic tirades, occurring in the midst of a longer speech:

> Perhaps in fact it is better that all the things you people did would happen, that tens of thousands would be slaughtered and hundreds of thousands would be exiled. Aren't the Jews

here one big refugee camp and the Arabs, too, one big refugee camp? So from now on the Arabs live out the catastrophe of their defeat day after day, and the Jews live out the revenge plotted against them night after night. Both peoples are consumed with hatred and venom, and both of them will emerge from the war suffused with vengeful impulses and self-righteousness. And from all the whole rivers of vengeance and self-righteousness the entire country is covered with graveyards and sown with the ruins of hundreds of miserable villages that once existed and were utterly wiped out.

The power of these words is evident. They are framed by a writer who agonized over the bitter clash between the two peoples in Israel-Palestine and desperately sought a way of reconciliation. They are nothing that could be said in a court of public opinion in Israel, but they are enabled by the imaginative freedom of a novel, spoken as they are by a fictional character. They express not altogether what Amos Oz thought about the conflict but surely something he feared, something that haunted his nights.

What is remarkable about *Judas* is that this debate, with Gershom Wald a mostly implied counter to the Abravanel view, is given such a strong voice. The young protagonist more or less hovers between the two positions, listening to both. In any case, the somber question of who is thought to be a traitor casts a shadow over everything in the novel. Though Amos did not embrace the principled anti-Zionism of She'altiel Abravanel, he saw that the accusation of treason was wrong for such a man, actuated as he was by conscience, and the writer would surely have remembered that the labeling of Yitzhak Rabin as a traitor by many on the Israeli Right when he was working toward reconciliation with the Palestinians prepared the ground for his assassination.

One final point about *Judas* should be stressed. Abravanel, however much he aspired to avoid those rivers of blood, was a fanatic, for the novelist who invented him understood that one can be a fanatic for the avoidance of conflict just as one can be a fanatic for militant nationalism. Fanaticism of any sort entails an insistence that the facts of historical circumstance must conform to the advocated ideology, even when they manifestly do not. The rivers of blood shed from 1947—actually from 1921—to the present are horrific, as Atalia, like her late father, says, but it is hard to see how they could have been avoided, how the Jews and the Arabs could have lived together in a peaceable reality beyond nationality, how the endangered Zionist community would not have been slaughtered and the survivors exiled if the attacks launched against it in 1947 had not been met with armed force. Amos, who from his Jerusalem childhood had looked hard into the seething cauldron of irreconcilable differences among the adherents of Zionism, had a deep understanding of these unyielding differences, and one of his distinctive contributions as a writer was to give them compelling expression in his fiction. The uncertainty of this novel's conclusion, intended as an open ending, in which Shmuel Asch leaves the Abravanel home and heads to the Negev for an undefined future, may well be an oblique reflection of how this political argument remains unresolved. Nevertheless, for a novelist so profoundly engaged in the terrible challenges of his nation's political realm, *Judas* was a fitting last act.

The fiction of Amos Oz, as we have seen, is firmly anchored in the Israeli setting and in the distinctive Israeli experience. But good fiction can illuminate the endless variety of possible human types with all their psychological quirks and contradictions, their effects on others, their entanglements in class, culture, and ideology. Amos was able to do this in one book after another, though, inevitably, not with the same degree of success in each. Late in life, for example, he himself had doubts about *Black Box* (1987) and *To Know a Woman* (1989), doubts that I felt as well when I read both novels upon their appearance. The vehemence of the critical attacks on these books certainly was wounding and has no real analogue in American literary life. Under banner headlines, his writing was denounced as fake, empty, pure kitsch. The ever-hostile Dan Miron dismissed his fiction as hopelessly narcissistic and worthless, its author capable only of performing the opera of himself.

There are clearly lapses in the novels of Amos Oz, as there are in the works of most writers. Nevertheless, the range of human types in his novels and stories is striking and explains in part why his books have appealed to readers in many countries who may have no special interest in Israel's political and social predicaments. Atalia in *Judas* is just one example of his range. He had never before invented a female character with her peculiar mix of bitterness, imperiousness, enigmatic self-presentation, and potent but elusive sexuality. I am not sure whether he ever met a woman like her, but novelists create characters not only from observation but also from deep places in their psyche. Atalia, after all, perfectly embodies the combination of tantalizing allure and elusiveness that was his own perception of woman as an object of male desire. Beyond projection of this kind, Amos repeatedly spoke of himself as a spy on the people he spotted around him, going all the way back to those he observed when his parents took him to a café to meet with friends, where the silenced child scanned the space around him and invented biographies, character traits, vocations, likes and dislikes, for each person he saw. Such imaginative inventions went on almost to the end, and they explain in part why he was a thoroughly Israeli writer who managed to be more than an Israeli writer.

From what literary background did Amos's writing emerge? Modern Hebrew literature was naturally an important resource and frame of reference. Even as Amos avoided emulating Agnon, the brilliant older writer was an inspiration. The haunting novella *In the Prime of Her Life*, which begins with the story of a woman who dies young, told by her adult daughter, who has a troubled memory of her mother, lost early, spoke directly to Amos for biographical reasons, but many other Agnon stories and novels informed his imaginative world. Two early twentieth-century Hebrew novelists especially engaged him—Y. H. Brenner, who represented the moral failings of his Jewish contemporaries, first in eastern Europe and then in Palestine, with ruthless honesty, and M. D. Berdichevsky, who never moved to Palestine from the European settings where he wrote novels and stories abounding in situations in which primal urges, especially sexual ones, rip through the fabric of conventional morality.

Amos also immersed himself in the work of many foreign writers, which for the most part he read in Hebrew translations. The Russians—Chekhov, Tolstoy, Dostoevsky (the last also an influence on Brenner)—exerted a special magnetism, and he addressed Chekhov, perhaps the most important figure for him, directly in some of his nonfiction. Among English-language writers, in addition to Sherwood Anderson, both Joyce and Faulkner spoke to him through their fiction, although, unlike the response to them by A. B. Yehoshua, there is scant indication in his own writing that he was drawn to adopt their techniques of interior monologue. Once he began his far-flung travels abroad, he had occasion to meet writers at various international literary festivals, which he surely enjoyed, but the one foreign novelist with whom he established a real friendship was the Peruvian Mario Vargas Llosa, who was close to him in age. Again, there are no signs of "influence," but it was meaningful for him to have as a friend someone from across the world who was a writer of the first order of originality. In sum, Amos was very much part of the international literary world while always remaining a resolutely Israeli writer, rooted in his native soil and confronting its distinctive problems.

4

Friends, Family, and Performance

Amos Oz embraced three significant public roles as he made his way through life. In order of their importance for him they were: writer, political activist, and performer. Although political activism was certainly a higher priority for him than performance, I want to treat the latter first because his gifts as a performer fed into the way he implemented what we can justifiably call his mission as an activist. How these three roles affected his interaction with people outside the public sphere is another question.

My sense is that Amos was in general more comfortable with groups than with all but a select few intimates. This is not to say that he had no aptitude for friendship. Over the years he acquired some devoted close friends, and these bonds were life-long. I have already mentioned Yisrael Tal, the general he met at the Hebrew University, who shepherded him through his military service, quite aware that he was not cut out to be a

combat soldier. He also enjoyed an enduring friendship with
the novelist Yehoshua Kenaz. Kenaz was a fine writer whose work
did not travel well in translation, in contrast to that of A. B.
Yehoshua, David Grossman, and Amos himself. Five of Kenaz's
books appeared in English, but they did not attract much of an
audience. I suspect the main reason might have been that the
major novel for which he was celebrated in Israel, *Infiltration*
(1986), which was widely read in Hebrew and established his
importance, is so deeply rooted in the Israeli army experience
that it is not easily accessible to readers elsewhere. He and Amos
became friends at the Hebrew University. He was almost the
same age as Amos. Like Amos, he was not a man suited to serve
at the front and ended up assigned to a unit for physically unfit
soldiers. Later he would be moved into intelligence. He died a
year and a half after Amos, at the age of eighty-three.

A friendship also developed with S. Yizhar, the major Hebrew novelist of the previous generation. He lived in Rehovot,
not very far from Hulda. Stylistically, Yizhar's fiction was quite
different from Amos's, for Amos never evinced much interest in
modernist innovations of form. Yizhar's twelve-hundred-page
novel *The Days of Ziklag* (1959), the central fictional stock-taking
of the emotional toll on Israeli youth of the fighting in 1948–
1949, was written in stream of consciousness, and when Yizhar
returned to fiction, after a decades-long silence, in the autobiographical *Preliminaries* (1992), he again resorted largely to stream
of consciousness. One astute American reader of my acquaintance who read it in translation aptly called it a late modernist
masterpiece. Whatever the differences in the kind of novels
they wrote, Amos keenly admired Yizhar's work, and politically
there was much that drew the two together. Yizhar, too, was a
liberal Zionist—in fact, a member of the Zionist establishment—
who provided a voice of conscience in Israel, not refraining
from unblinking criticism of Israeli treatment of Arabs even in
the heat of the War of Independence. Yizhar and Amos saw each

other frequently. There were gatherings of intellectuals at Yizhar's home in Rehovot on Friday nights, and when Amos was able to commandeer a kibbutz car, he and Nily made the short drive to attend them. Amos was at Yizhar's bedside in his last days.

Among Israeli writers on the Left, Amos was a warm friend of David Grossman. The bonds of intimacy between both of them and A. B. Yehoshua made the three a kind of literary-political trio. This friendship may seem a bit surprising to American readers. After all, relations among such American writers as Norman Mailer, Philip Roth, Bernard Malamud, and John Updike were chiefly marked by rivalry, not friendship. The difference may have something to do with Israel's being a small country with a vital literary culture. The Hebrew writers surely shared some sense that they were partners in creating a new Hebrew literature; indeed, a case can be made that the extraordinary revival of Hebrew and the shaping of a vibrant Hebrew literature were the most fully successful aspect of the Zionist revolution. Although the personalities involved have to count for much, this engagement in a common national culture may explain in part why the writers were able to feel such warmth and mutual support in their relationships.

Beyond Israel, Amos had one important personal connection. In 1969–1970, he was invited to be a visiting fellow at the Oxford Centre for Hebrew and Jewish Studies. After arriving in England with his wife and his two young daughters, he went to introduce himself to the British philosopher and intellectual historian Isaiah Berlin, who welcomed him warmly, and the two of them, the young novelist and the eminent professor, became fast friends. Berlin, a Zionist with a broad humanistic outlook, was not hesitant to voice criticism of militant nationalism in Israel. Years later, Amos would write in a brief reminiscence of Berlin for *The Cambridge Companion to Isaiah Berlin*, "[He] taught me that one could be national without being nationalist, and patriotic without loathing or condescension for the patriotism of others. You can be a Zionist without ignoring Palestinian justice." Berlin's combination of urbanity and intellectual seriousness strongly appealed to Amos. When Amos's daughter Fania spent six years at Oxford for her graduate studies, Berlin, though then retired, took it upon himself to serve as a mentor for her. Amos frequently visited Oxford to see Fania during those years and always happily engaged in conversation with Berlin. He read at least some of Berlin's work, finding in it a philosophical underpinning for his own political views. A phrase from Kant that Berlin liked to invoke, "the crooked timber of humanity," was especially resonant for Amos: that humanity, Amos felt, was "the seed of liberty, but also the sap of literature."

Not long after the time in Oxford, Amos became close friends with Nurith Gertz, who was married to Amos Kenan, a popular journalist in Israel and the author of a couple of sensationalist novels with political messages, a man who had swung from the extremist Right to the extremist Left. Nurith is a prominent critic of Israeli literature and film.

Nurith became one of the chief witnesses, beyond Amos's immediate family, to his last months. During that time she had frequent conversations with him by phone and in person that included certain important revelations of his feelings about his life. She transcribed some of these exchanges from her recordings in a Hebrew book called *What Was Lost*, published two years after his death. Although Nurith Gertz is an excellent writer, this book is a bit unsteady in its focus: it is subtitled "Biography of a Friendship," but it vacillates between being a biography and being a fragmentary autobiography and a series of reflections on her late husband, with certain affinities proposed between him and Amos Oz that are rather questionable. In any event, her reports about her conversations with Amos are a valuable source for understanding what sort of person he was.

The two became acquainted when Nurith Gertz was writing an M.A. thesis on him and sought him out. They met for coffee, felt a mutual rapport, and before long were close friends who would remain in frequent contact over the years. The ever-busy rumor mills in Israel concluded that they were lovers—to judge by photos, Nurith was a very attractive young woman—but she is careful not to give the slightest hint of such a relationship in her book. She often visited Amos and Nily at Hulda with her young daughters, making a sometime romantic connection unlikely though not inconceivable. Whatever the case, their friendship remained sufficiently intimate that Amos felt he could confide in her at a time when he knew his days were numbered. There were, I should add, a good many rumors about Amos's other possible affairs, but I will not speculate here on their accuracy.

Did Nily have any suspicions about their relationship? I would never have asked her, though one of her women friends might have passed on the rumors to her, which could have introduced a certain note of strain in their loving relationship. But the solidity of their marriage was clearly never shaken, and the tribute Amos paid to Nily on her sixtieth birthday and then in a conversation with Nurith Gertz toward the end of his life seems heartfelt. Even if Amos might have engaged in extramarital activities, Nily certainly had a justified sense that she remained, after all, the important woman in his life. At the very end, he was still celebrating her as the radiant presence that had brightened his world for sixty years.

More is known with certainty about Amos's friendships with men. Beyond the relationships already mentioned, he developed one close friendship with someone from the scientific community. Marek Glezerman, who had emigrated to Israel from Germany in the early 1970s, was a recently appointed professor of obstetrics and gynecology at Ben-Gurion University when Amos joined the faculty there in the later 1980s. He was more than an ordinary professor of medicine, for he would go on to gain international renown as a pioneer of gender- and sex-conscious medicine, with multiple publications in the field and frequent invitations to teach abroad. His intellectual power as well as his area of specialization would surely have drawn Amos to him, but it is also very likely that Amos, who often celebrated curiosity as a key moral value in human relations and in the writing of fiction, was fascinated to know someone whose rigorous scientific perspective on the world was so different from his literary one.

Amos's loyal devotion to a few friends suggests that he did not lack a readiness for intimate friendship, yet many people felt he was a little stiff or even somewhat unnatural in one-on-one encounters. Someone who had a passing acquaintance with him told me that when they were together, he felt that Amos would have been more comfortable being alone, at his desk, working on his novels. A writer's vocation can be a lonely one, perhaps especially for novelists, who may need long stretches of time to carry out their large projects. Amos could exercise a distinct social charm, but there was a core of aloneness as he balanced the task of writing and the necessity of social relations.

My own friendship with Amos always seemed to me perfectly comfortable, perhaps because we shared many literary enthusiasms and political views. When he first came to Berkeley in 1970, he was as eager to meet me after I had written about him as I was to meet him. Given the geographical distance between Israel and the west coast of the United States, the times we spent together were few and far between, but I felt a sense of personal warmth whenever we did get together. However, I recall one meeting that confirmed the perception of his being somehow constrained in his interaction with others who were not his closest intimates. More than thirty years ago, we were at a conference together in Jerusalem, the topic of which now escapes me. During a break between sessions, he and I stood at the back of the large lecture hall, at that moment mostly emptied, in deep conversation. We were talking about what one so often talks about in Israel, the Situation (*hamatzav*), a subject of urgent interest to both of us. But as Amos laid out his views on the conflict with Palestinians, I began to get the slightly eerie impression that in speaking to me he was addressing an audience of hundreds. (Perhaps the political topic triggered a reflexive flip into his on-stage mode.) I had a sense that he may have been somehow caught, perhaps even trapped, in his role as public performer. Some years later, when I first read *A Tale of Love and Darkness* and came upon the report of how his parents would trot out their precocious and attractive only child to display his talents before guests, I had an insight into the source of this continuing embrace of performance as a default mode for relating to people.

If the gossips had sundry suspicions about Amos, there was also a general perception of him as a husband and father deeply attached to his family. He was devoted to Nily and always cherished her as a bright presence in his life, someone with a temperament in many ways antithetical to his own. His public tribute to her at Arad in 1999 is touching and seems perfectly sincere. He cared about his three children, and two of them, Fania and Daniel, would, as adults, continue to show their great love and admiration for him. But barely two years after his death, in February 2021, a familial bombshell exploded that shook public opinion in Israel, generating sadness and distress, certainly for the family, as well as for many others. Unfortunately, it cannot be skipped over here because it has to be factored into any assessment of Amos's character.

Galia, the younger of Amos's two daughters, was known to have been estranged from him for the last seven years of his life, although she did not publicly reveal her reasons for it. The estrangement was acutely painful for Amos. In a passage from Nurith's book that was cut at Galia's insistence before the published version appeared, Amos told Nurith, "It's a knife not only thrust in but constantly twisting." Galia felt so alienated from her father that she refused to visit him when he was dying and did not come to his public funeral. Her book, *Something That Pretends to Be Love*, is a fierce denunciation of her father. In her account, he repeatedly abused her as a child, verbally and physically, frequently beating her and heaping humiliating insults on her. She does not hesitate to call him a violent man and a sadist. Needless to say, this description constitutes an extreme reversal of the way he was generally perceived in his lifetime. The initial response of Nily, Fania, and Daniel was tactfully discreet: her pain is real, they said several times, but we remember things differently. (Daniel was not yet born when Galia was growing up.) Reactions in Israel to Galia's denunciation of her father were, predictably, sharply divided. Some Israelis found it quite unbelievable; others took Galia at her word, whether because they had always harbored reservations about Amos Oz or because they were following the widespread inclination in the era of #MeToo to give credence to any woman who says she has been victimized. No outsider can ever know for sure what actually transpired in the Oz family at Hulda. As one Israeli novelist who was a friend of Amos's wrote to me, every person, after all, has a dark side. However, a few things may be sorted out, at least in an assessment based on likelihood, and this should be done because the whole troubling affair is bound to affect our perception of what sort of person Amos was.

Scathing accusations like Galia's probably do not emerge from a complete vacuum. The available indications do point to a context of tensions between father and daughter when she was growing up. Galia's claim, however, that Amos was a violent man seems on the face of it questionable. Fania, in the wake of the storm stirred up by her sister, said that she herself witnessed just two occasions on which her father acted violently toward her sister, one when he forcefully pushed her out of their kibbutz apartment and another when he verbally abused her. Both occasions were shocking, even traumatic, for Fania. She never observed any beatings, despite her sister's claim that she had black and blue marks she had to hide. Fania also firmly dismissed her sister's contention that she saw Amos hitting Nily, and from what is known about the marriage, even though it may have been marked by occasional vehement arguments, as most marriages, even happy ones, are, it is unlikely he ever exhibited violence toward her. But Fania also writes that her sister was very provocative, both as a child and as an adult, exhibiting an almost preternatural ability to wound with words; she was verbally aggressive toward the other members of the family to the point of intimidating all three of them. In a harsh confrontation between the sisters when they were in their twenties, Fania felt so humiliated and verbally assaulted by Galia that she was afraid to see her for a long time afterward. In sum, it is reasonable to conclude that all was not peaceful in the Oz family and that Amos could have been driven to lose control by a child who, at least according to her sister's testimony, could be difficult. There were at least two such instances, as Fania notes, and perhaps somewhat more frequently if less vehemently in things he said to her. He confessed in a late interview to throwing coffee—presumably not scalding coffee—at her and on at least one occasion slapping her.

I cannot say with absolute confidence that Galia's scathing accusations could not possibly be true—even loving parents may occasionally lose control under provocation from a child and then keenly regret it—but possibility is not probability. The evidence that has surfaced does not warrant the conclusion that Amos Oz, the peace advocate, the proponent of measured reason, and the engaging social presence was a raging, punitive man beneath the surface. What is not a matter of dispute is that Galia's break with him cast a deep shadow over his last seven years. Why she chose that moment to initiate the break is still another piece of this jagged-edged puzzle. She was in her fifties and had continued to join the family for holiday celebrations and other occasions over the years. Also, one might assume that if she were so alienated from her father, she would not have retained the last name he had invented for himself. Her sister, devoted as she was to their father, chose to add her husband's name on the other side of a hyphen from "Oz." Why, moreover, as her sister notes, did she often leave her two children to stay with Amos and Nily if she knew her father to be a violently abusive parent?

Alas, controversy in Israel over Galia's accusatory book still rages. A kind of posthumous boycott of Amos and his work seems to be underway. A recently published list of Israeli authors recommended for inclusion in school curricula leaves out his name. When a launch was scheduled in early 2022 at the Tzavta Club in Tel Aviv for a small volume of Nily's taped reminiscences of Amos, one prominent Israeli novelist refused to take part in an event celebrating a writer who, he said, had abused his daughter. The unwarranted certainty of this declaration is alarming. Having watched Galia in an hour-long interview on Israeli television, I think she fully believes everything she has said about her father, but that hardly proves things happened just as she claims. Amos clearly had a troubled relationship with his child, who, at least on the testimony of her sister, could be provocative. Amos deeply regretted, as he said publicly, the times he lost control with her. But the anguish he felt during his last seven years over her estrangement from him is testimony to his continuing love for her, and his complete bafflement about her implacable withdrawal from him indicates that to him, at least as he remembered whatever had gone on when she was a child, her total alienation was very hard to explain. "What was I guilty of?" were his words in a late interview. His relationship with his older daughter, as she attests in a brief memoir of him, was very loving and marked by intellectual sharing, and he certainly comes across as a father who felt deep affection for all three of his children.

In any case, Amos, beginning in 1969, when Fania was eight

and Galia was five, would periodically be away from the family for weeks at a time as he launched the long series of travels abroad that continued until two years before his death. Surprisingly, the first time he ventured outside Israel, apart from the ill-fated visit to his father in England at the age of sixteen, was when he was thirty. *My Michael* initially appeared in Hebrew in the spring of 1968 and quickly moved into additional printings; translations began to appear the following year. It proved to be an international bestseller, and the high esteem in which this novel was widely held did not diminish over the years—it was even included in one listing by a German publisher of the hundred most important novels written in the twentieth century. As time went on, Amos would be showered with awards and honors across the globe, from France (the Legion of Honor), Germany, Italy, Spain, Norway, and Russia to South Korea. In fact, he received so many prizes that the writer of the NB column that appears on the back page of the *Times Literary Supplement* could not resist a satiric jibe at the surfeit of awards. These prizes are worth mentioning because what went along with them was a constant stream of invitations to appear for lectures and interviews. Amos ended up traveling to five continents, sometimes with Nily, more often by himself. And even when he was at home in Israel, he was repeatedly asked to speak in public forums and at institutions of higher learning.

Amos appears to have been happy to accept the many invitations to give talks, whether about his own writing or on political issues, because he discovered that he keenly enjoyed doing the public presentations, and it was an activity that energized him. Promoting himself and his work surely would also have been a motive. I witnessed the invigorating effect of his public appearances the last time I saw him, in November 2016, two years before his death. He was speaking to a packed house in the large auditorium of the San Francisco Jewish Community Center about his novel *Judas*, which had just appeared in English translation. (We were able to talk privately for only a few minutes after his talk.) When Amos appeared on the stage, he looked frail, visibly weakened by the disease and the chemotherapy he had undergone. I wondered, Why is he doing this at all? I got my answer when he began to speak. All of a sudden he was lively, energetic, beguiling as he had always been in addressing audiences. I realized that the hundreds of listeners in that hall, captivated by everything he was saying, offered the oxygen he needed to breathe, the powerful stimulus that made him very much alive even as he was dying. At that point, he certainly did not need the sale of multiple copies of the book or any honorarium he might have received for the talk, but he did need the audience.

The talented child in the Kerem Avraham apartment who was asked by his parents to perform was still performing, almost to the end. These performances have to be described in this narrative because they were such an important part of his life. There is no point in trying to follow chronologically the countless scores of talks he gave across the globe for almost fifty years. Instead, I will offer two representative snapshots. One is of a Hebrew talk he gave in Israel, the other of a lecture in Australia. As I shall try to show, there were certain notable differences in how he gauged his audience and addressed it at home and abroad. The way he presented himself and his ideas in public—in these talks and, as we shall see, in his political talks—is important for understanding who he was and what the nature of the positions he espoused was.

The different languages he used in his talks made a difference. The few talks by Amos I heard in America were in English. His English (the only language besides Hebrew that he spoke) was completely fluent, his foreignness to the language marked only by a certain Israeli accent and an occasional slip in idiomatic usage. These were by no means an impediment to his effectiveness, and he was perfectly comfortable speaking in English even without a prepared text. I first heard him lecture in Hebrew at an event honoring him upon his retirement from Ben-Gurion University. I, among others, had been invited to speak, too. His performance in Hebrew was a revelation. With scant reference to notes, he emitted an uninterrupted flow of improvised eloquence. He seemed to have on tap all the riches, all the nuances and subtleties, all the vivid idiomatic coloration of the Hebrew language, and to be able to deploy them at will, apparently without premeditated calculation.

The Hebrew talk I shall report on, which I watched on You-Tube, was given at the Weizmann Institute of Science in February 2013. In contrast to the retirement event at Ben-Gurion University, which was held in a large auditorium, this involved a rather modest gathering, with perhaps fifty or sixty people, mostly middle-aged or older, seated on folding chairs under a tent or canopy. Other events appear to have been going on at the same time at the Weizmann Institute: in the middle of the talk, I could see a wedding party passing by outside; the bride, dressed in the expected white gown, stopped to pose for the photographer.

At the beginning of the lecture, Amos was seated behind a table; within a few minutes, in order to make better contact with the audience, he came around to the front of the table and sat on it. The context, then, encouraged a certain informality in the presentation, although the modest size of the group by no means diminished his energy or his manifest effort to engage his listeners. Amos had a small sheet of notes in front of him but looked down at it only occasionally. Given the nature of the event, his Hebrew was a somewhat more relaxed colloquial language, with fewer traces of the "Shabbat Hebrew," with which he was so adept, than were manifest in his addresses to larger Israeli audiences. For some reason he was also speaking quite rapidly, perhaps because he felt he had a lot of material to squeeze into the sixty minutes allotted to him. His subject on this occasion was literary, not political, dealing first with the general topic of reading—reading fiction in particular—and then with his process as a writer.

What is strikingly evident in this talk, as in all his lectures and public appearances, is his gift for getting across what he wanted to say through lively, concrete, and often homey examples. To characterize, for instance, the typically female reader of the nineteenth-century European novel, he explains that she had to be of a certain class, with the nanny tending to the children in the nursery, the maid in the kitchen preparing dinner, another household servant sweeping up and dusting the furniture, while the imagined female reader was comfortably ensconced on a sofa or in an easy chair, her copy of Balzac or George Eliot in hand. Then, to show what an unusual and peculiar experience reading literature is, unlike experiencing any of the other arts, he defamiliarizes it. Imagine, he proposes, a space traveler arriving on earth from another planet; the extraterrestrial visitor looks at the page of an open book and sees on it rows of what seem to him to be dead ants. What he cannot fathom, coming as he does from elsewhere, is that the reader is able to imbue the dead ants in his or her imagination with teeming life, to enter into a story that includes adulterous passion, jealousy, guilt pangs, impulses of vengeance, not to speak of ballrooms, gleaming satin gowns, living rooms crowded with heavily upholstered furniture, and also locomotives, carriages, and perhaps even a pistol or a vial of poison. (The concrete illustrations here are mine, not Amos's, but they are very much in the spirit of his presentation.)

Another technique he adopts to vivify his explanations is to use analogy. Reading, he says, is always an intimate relationship of two, the reader and the book, so it is like making love—no reader's experience can be identical with another's, and to have the proper experience, the reader must be fully there, as in lovemaking. Amos cinches the point with a pungent personal recollection. Once, when he was about to get in bed with a woman who was lying naked in what she must have assumed was an enticing pose, she said to him, "Surprise me." This in effect reduced the twosome to a pairing of one and a half. She had made herself a passive participant, almost a kind of sex doll. In contrast, reading has to be a full engagement of both parties, between the printed words on the page artfully wrought by the writer and the imaginatively participating reader. The analogy may be imprecise, but Amos as a speaker was inclined to go for such comparisons precisely because they were likely to captivate his audience.

To this general account of what goes into reading, Amos appends a proposition about what good fiction should be like. Faithful to the lesson he had learned early on from Sherwood Anderson that led him to write about the kibbutz, he argues that all great literature is provincial, for we all inescapably live in one province or another. Even a novel about a vast metropolis cannot really deal with the broad expanses of the city but has to zero in on a neighborhood or street defined by those who live there through their own distinctive provincial practices. It is through the provincial, Amos says, speaking from his own experience as a novelist, that a writer attains the universal. At the same time he wants to make clear to his audience that in depicting a given milieu a writer is necessarily reimagining and transforming it, not making a photographic reproduction of it. He introduces another of his homey personal anecdotes by way of illustration. There was a kibbutz member who used to comb his hair whenever he came into the room where Amos was writing. When Amos asked him about this, he explained, "Well, if you put me in your story, I want to look my best." The wonderful absurdity of this idea reflects Amos's knack for explaining his ideas in beguiling and often humorous ways.

From reading and the nature of fiction, the talk proceeds to a depiction of Amos's practice as a writer. Some of what he says repeats notions that appear in *A Tale of Love and Darkness*. As a child, he proposes, he became a fiction writer by being a spy. His parents sometimes took him along when they were meeting friends at a café. On these occasions, he was under strict orders to sit quietly and never interrupt. To amuse himself during this imposed silence, he became a spy, scanning the faces and attire of people at other tables and inventing stories about who they were, their likes and dislikes, their professions, their personal attachments. He has remained, he suggests, this kind of spy ever since, and out of the spying he has made his stories and novels. The child's curiosity became the novelist's curiosity, and elsewhere he repeatedly affirmed curiosity as a positive moral value.

Other piquant observations on his experience as a writer emerge in the talk. About the kibbutz as subject: when you remove the gap between, say, the rich girl and the poor girl through the economic egalitarianism instituted by the collective, what is laid bare is more existential disparities—for example, between the pretty girl and the one who is irredeemably unattractive. Amos also says that his subject has always been the family— he said that in at least one interview about *A Tale of Love and Darkness*—but, in keeping with the famous first sentence of *Anna Karenina*, his subject has always been the unhappy family. What generates interest for the writer and his readers is, as he puts it in concrete terms, the family as it creaks, cracks, shudders, gives off smoke, yet somehow continues to chug along. The kibbutz constitutes a kind of extended family, and in his fiction, it is manifestly an unhappy one.

Watching this talk at the Weizmann Institute, one sees Amos's delight in charming his audience, in entertaining them as he conveys ideas about writing, reading, and literature that were important to him. And as he addresses a group of fellow Israelis in their common language who have read him in Hebrew, there is a kind of ease and familiarity that are absent in his lectures in English to audiences abroad. In any case, he loved having an audience, he was probably more comfortable with an audience than with most individual interlocutors, and he wanted and needed to have one. His pleasure in addressing groups also explains why he was happy to embrace his belated career as a university teacher of literature.

My other snapshot from Amos's lecturing career is of a talk, which I also watched on YouTube, that he gave two years later at Monash University in Melbourne, roughly a year and a half after the diagnosis of cancer. His daughter Fania was a visiting professor there, and she introduced him graciously and affectionately to the large audience. The subject was Israel—what kind of country it was—and then, toward the end, Amos presented his views on how the long conflict with the Palestinians had to be resolved. The first part of the talk would have been entirely superfluous for an Israeli audience, and the second part would have been redundant in Israel in another way: he was spelling out a position he had aired again and again in Israel, both in public forums and in articles in the press.

It was certainly reasonable for him to assume that perceptions of Israel from abroad were compounded of misleading notions picked up from the media and sheer ignorance, so, as in most of his talks to English-speaking groups, he aimed to provide a sense of the cultural vitality of the country and the full variety of its clashing viewpoints. Israel, he proposes to those gathered, is a nation created by dreamers—he notes, pointedly, that nothing is more devastating to the allure of a dream than its partial and necessarily imperfect realization—but the dreams of the creators were always in conflict with each other. (He repeated this idea in many of his talks abroad.) He then launches into a set piece. Some of the dreamers imagined re-creating in Palestine a vibrant version of Central European *Bürgerlichkeit*, with operas and theaters, with cafés where one could sit and drink coffee *mit Schlag*. Others imagined a revival of biblical Israel, or a through-and-through Marxist state, or an agrarian socialist community in the spirit of Tolstoy, or a reincarnation of the old eastern European *shtetl*. This is accurate enough and explains in part the disorderly politics of Israel today, which Amos very likely had in mind. But he goes on to a move that is characteristic of the way he addressed audiences outside Israel, which I would call didactic hyperbole. The media, he contends, gives you a picture of Israel as a country made up of 80 percent settlers, 19 percent ruthless soldiers, and 1 percent leftist intellectuals. A less generous rubric for this style of explanation would be caricature. In the same spirit, to get across the idea that Israel is a society of endless debate, which he construes as a sign of its healthiness, he proposes that every bus stop constitutes a kind of impromptu seminar where the people waiting for their bus vehemently argue opposing views. I suppose streetside discussions might occasionally happen, and it is true that Israelis tend to be more uninhibitedly vocal than people in Anglophone societies, but at most Israeli bus stops the passengers wait in silence for the arrival of the bus, just as they do elsewhere. This silence does not gainsay the general contention that Israel is, in the formula used in the talk, "a civilization of doubt and disagreement." Amos backs this statement up with a personal anecdote—his lectures, as I have already noted, are often enlivened by such anecdotes. During the 1973 war, while the frontline unit in which he was serving was preparing for a battle with the Syrians, the general commanding the forces in the north paid a visit to his unit and before long became engaged in a vigorous debate with some of the soldiers about Tolstoy's *War and Peace*. It is hard to imagine that happening in the American army or, I presume, in the Australian army.

Nevertheless, the popularizing flourishes of Amos's lectures to audiences abroad did lead to certain simplifications. Thus, when Abraham bargains with God over how many righteous people in Sodom would be required to avert the divine decree of destruction, Amos said he was arguing "like a shrewd second-hand car dealer." Here, as in other instances, he compromised accuracy for the sake of vividness. On some broader issues, the inclination to frame things for easy absorption by a popular audience sometimes slides into oversimplification. In the Monash University talk, in keeping with those purported seminars at bus stops, Amos characterizes not just Israel but Jews all the way back to biblical origins as constituting "a civilization of doubt and argument." There is surely a grain of truth in this—as Amos goes on to say, there never could have been a Jewish pope dictating principles of faith and practice to the adherents of Judaism. Yet there were also many manifestations of repression of dissent during the long course of Jewish history. Spinoza voiced doubt and disagreement in his writings, and the Jewish community of Amsterdam responded by excommunicating him for life; they never considered debating his challenging ideas. In the next two centuries, as Hasidism spread through eastern Europe, its Jewish opponents sometimes denounced the Hasidim to civil authorities as dangerous subversives who should be jailed, and in certain instances they excommunicated them without any debate. Jews often argued with other Jews, but the practice of debate should not be idealized, for Jews often were also intransigently intolerant of Jews who thought differently.

When Amos turns in this Monash University lecture to the conflict with the Palestinians, his rhetorical strategy shifts. Much of what he says is what he would say, and did say, to Israeli audiences. The vividly accessible plain language is deployed here as well, but without the didactic hyperbole of his portrayal of Israel and of Judaism. He uses one trope that he repeatedly invoked in his talks on the conflict in Israel, real estate and housing: the Israelis and the Palestinians are two families between whom there are bitter differences; they cannot possibly live in the same house (the one-state solution), so they will have to settle for a duplex home, with a solid partition separating the two domiciles. In a complementary metaphor, he calls the conflict "a real estate dispute" that has to be settled through compromise.

Notably, the segment of the talk devoted to the conflict is much less dependent on hyperbolic metaphors and analogies. Instead, Amos makes abundant use of direct, unadorned assertion: The Israelis and the Palestinians are both there because neither has anywhere else to go. For each, the division of the disputed territory will be experienced as a painful amputation, for many in each group passionately feel that all of it belongs to them. As the basis for compromise, each of the two peoples must come to the sober recognition that "we are not alone in this country." As Amos bluntly remarks in this talk, "You make peace with an enemy," not because you love him, for after all, he has long been your enemy, but because he is the one with whom you have to make peace. This was Amos's deep conviction from the aftermath of the 1967 war to the end of his life, and he argued for it in much the same way to Israelis and to people abroad, without public-relations strategies.

Amos remained an optimist throughout his life. Absent a core of optimism, an advocate of reconciliation can scarcely persist in the face of a reality that seems to be a hopelessly lethal clash between uncompromising forces. He concludes his Monash lecture by conjuring up an optimistic alternative to the current dire state of affairs. In his depiction of an Israel earlier in his talk as a country that is different from the way it is seen in the media, he emphasized the Israel of the coastal plain, which gets scant attention in public representations of the country. This Israel encompasses hundreds of thousands of predominantly secular, mostly middle-class Jews who are not fierce nationalists and who aspire to enjoy the cultural resources and the material comforts of the larger modern world—the Israel, I would say by way of illustration, of Eurovision, of booming high tech, film, and television, of the internationally acclaimed works of Amichai, David Grossman, and many others.

In the conclusion of the lecture, Amos expresses hope for a time when Israel will occupy and annex not territory but the literary supplements, the arts sections, the scientific sections of papers around the world. In point of fact, an efflorescence of culture, science, and technology has been taking place even in the midst of chronic political disarray and purblind policies and actions that have done grave damage to Palestinians and to Israelis alike. The novels and stories of Amos Oz have been a prominent part of the efflorescence.

To understand Amos's life, it is important to have in mind a concrete sense of his performances at the lectern because from the time he attained international fame around the age of thirty, such performances took up a large portion of his professional activities. This was true to a good extent even at home in Israel, but the globe-trotting lectures consumed considerably more time and energy. To cite one example, after the appearance of *A Tale of Love and Darkness* in more than forty languages, he gave many dozens of talks and interviews on that book at venues ranging from North America to western Europe, Scandinavia, and even the Far East. In some cases, the presentations were part of promotional tours, but such author appearances mostly have a modest effect on sales, and in any case, once Amos had moved from Hulda to Arad and was no longer depositing his royalties into the kibbutz kitty, he enjoyed a very ample income from his books. If you ask yourself why a man in his sixties would fling himself into a strenuous schedule that involved flying around the world, the conclusion has to be that he needed to bask in the limelight and feel the pleasure and satisfaction of exercising his gift for charming, entertaining, and instructing rapt audiences. Moreover, he certainly would have been impelled by a desire to enhance his reputation far and wide, even if that might not have been his principal motive in going.

Did all his author appearances and travels affect his writing? As far as I can tell, not in the least. Writing was essentially an activity opposite to his relaxed, almost seductive improvisations from notes in the lectures, his captivating and at times facile illustrations and analogies and personal anecdotes. In contrast, the kind of writing to which he was uncompromisingly committed involved painstaking labor with language, character, and plot, a constant effort to get all the components of the novel or story just right. In the talk at the Weizmann Institute, he likens his work as a writer to the delicate procedure of a watchmaker: each word has to be picked up with small pincers, held to the light, and scrutinized to determine whether it will fit precisely into the gears of the fictional device. This sounds rather like Flaubert's pursuit as a novelist of *le mot juste*, which may not be how the relation of Amos Oz to the writer's calling is commonly perceived.

The painstaking aspect of his writing process is documented in the taped interviews he did with Shira Hadad, the editor who became a friend and then an intelligent interlocutor, in the last year and a half of his life. These were published in Hebrew as a short book entitled *What's in an Apple?* scant months before his death. They also provide an instructive glimpse into his deepest feelings about life and death. What he stressed here about his writing is that he constantly used multiple drafts for episodes in his novels, often four or more, sometimes even ten. He put these alternative drafts in a drawer, then reread them and decided which worked best, or whether he needed to do something different. *Judas* has one historical chapter, his narrative of the crucifixion. He explained to Shira Hadad that his first draft came to sixty pages, the second to eighty. He threw away draft after draft and in the end came up with a version he felt he could live with that took up just twelve and a half pages. This process is quite similar to Flaubert's in writing *Madame Bovary:* he cut down his manuscript from an initial draft of close to 3,000 manuscript pages to produce a beautifully wrought book of 250 printed pages, the very model of the art-novel.

So the public appearances did not undermine Amos's rigorous craft as a novelist, although they may have provided a certain relief from the rigors of writing, enabling him to win over audiences not through slow, patient work but through easier improvisation, through the sheer projection of his engaging public presence.

There was one exception to this sharp division between lecturing and writing. When he was in his early seventies, he collaborated with his daughter Fania on a book called *Jews and Words*, written in English and published in 2012 by Yale University Press. The fact that it was written in English in itself points to a connection in the framing of its argument with the characteristic procedure of his lectures to popular audiences around the world, which were always given in English. The aim of the book is to offer an overview of Jewish culture from biblical times to the present, demonstrating the constant commitment to language as the vehicle of ideas and values and as the principal manifestation of the distinctive character of the culture. Fania Oz-Salzberger is a historian, so we might have hoped that this joining of the scrupulous methodology of the historian with the imaginative élan of the novelist would have produced a large view of Jewish culture that was both illuminating and engaging. For all the good intentions of the two authors, this for the most part was not the result they achieved. In French, a term, *haute vulgarisation*, "high popularization," denotes the popularization of a complex subject that manages to remain faithful to its complexities, to the thoroughness and precision with which it might be addressed in a more elaborate scholarly treatment. *Jews and Words* unfortunately tends to handle Jewish history and culture with somewhat simplifying generalizations that too often slip into apologetics.

The history of the Jews through the ages and in widespread geographical locations is a messy, disorderly, and contradictory business, and many manifestations are far from admirable. It is also unclear that a continuous line can be drawn from the Bible to all that follows because Judaism is as much a radical recasting and transformation of the biblical worldview and values as Christianity is. There are certainly brilliant cultural achievements and noble stances in the long vista of Jewish history, but most obscenities committed by gentiles—with the notable exception of genocide—have also been perpetrated by Jews, at least when they got the chance: the oppressive exercise of power, intolerance, exploitation of the poor and the helpless, even the murder of leaders, criminality of all kinds. Benya Krik, the mob boss of Isaac Babel's *Odessa Stories*, based on the writer's observation of an actual figure, is not a Jew of words, nor were Bugsie Siegal, Arnold Rothstein, Dutch Schultz, Meyer Lansky, and other Jews dealing in bullets, not words, during America's Prohibition Era. You would not guess any of this from *Jews and Words*. The book exhibits an unsettling continuity with the orally improvised images of Abraham as a used-car dealer and the Israeli bus stop as the venue for impromptu seminars. My guess is that Amos was encouraged to undertake this project with his daughter because of his experience at the lecture rostrum, and perhaps this collaboration was in some way a father's gesture of love for his daughter. But print, in contrast to oral presentation, is an unforgiving medium. Amos Oz knew this perfectly well when he was writing fiction, and it is just as well that he did not allow this single venture into popularized history to infiltrate his work as a novelist.

Early on, Amos had expressed a rather different view of Jewish history. In an essay he called "Like Gangsters on a Night of Long Knives, but a Little in a Dream," based on a radio talk he gave in 1978, he characterizes Jews through the ages as hysterically anxious, insecure about their standing in the world, and full of unearned self-congratulation. "We boast," he writes, "that we are the descendants of the Prophets, but we are really the descendants of the Jews who stoned the Prophets." At a later point in his life, after decades of appearances on the lecture rostrum around the world, he appears, in *Jews and Words*, to have temporarily swept this unblinking perception to the back of his consciousness.

Many writers have said writing is a lonely undertaking, and that, as I have observed, may be especially true for novelists. If we try to conceive how the parts of Amos Oz's life fit together, we can imagine a center with three concentric circles. The center is his writing, the novelist at his desk alone with the words he puts together and restlessly sifts through, words out of which he creates characters, a plot, a setting, and a whole world. It is this that Amos set out to do beginning in his childhood; this was the chief task he felt called on to perform in this life. The first circumambient sphere is the family, which was always dear to him despite painful struggles early and late with one of his two daughters and regardless of whether he may possibly have sometimes wandered from it. Then came the friends: his true intimates were perhaps few in number, but he was emotionally and intellectually nourished by them and remained steadfastly loyal to them over the years. The outer circle represents his engagement with groups, often large groups, as a performer. His public persona, unlike the spontaneous self interacting with family and close friends, was surely rooted in the person he really was but was also an artifact for public consumption, a studied projection. What this schema that I have sketched out does not include is Amos Oz as a political agent. The political self required public appearances, but it was very different from the performer promoting his books and painting a picture of Israel for non-Israelis.

5

·—◆—·

The Activist

FROM THE TIME Amos Oz came of age, he was passionately engaged in the nature and future of his troubled country and repeatedly sought to be a humane voice of reason in its highly contentious political debates. There was already an expression of that impulse when he was just twenty in his published rejoinder to Ben-Gurion on what needed to be the animating ideal of the kibbutz movement. After Israel's conquest of the West Bank and the Gaza Strip in 1967, these two areas of dense Palestinian population came under its control, and what to do about them has bedeviled Israel ever since. (Israel, we should remember, unilaterally withdrew from Gaza in 2005, evacuating Yamit, its settlement there, much to the outrage of one segment of Israelis. The subsequent domination of the Gaza Strip by Hamas, dedicated as it was and still is to the total destruction of Israel, has painfully demonstrated that the conflict between the two peoples has no simple solution.)

Amos's deep involvement in the public realm by no means sets him off from other Israeli writers. The two other figures who, with him, are arguably the outstanding Hebrew novelists of the past several decades, A. B. Yehoshua, his contemporary, and David Grossman, half a generation younger, have, like Amos, spoken out repeatedly on political questions, in articles and books and at public forums. In the sheer quantity of published political pieces, however, Amos probably goes beyond the other two. The 1987 collection of his opinion pieces, *The Slopes of Lebanon*, comprises forty-five articles, leaving out numerous briefer pieces, and an earlier miscellany, *In This Strong Blue Light*, includes many political pieces. These two books, moreover, appeared less than halfway through his career as a writer. There were times, he once estimated, when he was turning out two opinion articles a week.

In his many public appearances abroad, Amos often addressed political issues, and the views he expressed there were of course the same as those he expressed in his talks in Israel, though the talks abroad necessarily incorporated a kind of ABC of Israel and the nature of the conflict that would not have been necessary for his Israeli audiences. In any case, Israel itself was the real theater of his political activism. It was in Israel that he felt the urgent necessity to persuade through both the written and the spoken word. My impression is that he rarely turned down an invitation to speak on the issues, whether in academic settings, at public affairs institutions, or for popular audiences. He spoke publicly until the last year of his life, even when weakened by illness, making one last appearance at Tel Aviv University in June 2018, six months before his death. He did this because he was desperate to persuade, although in his last months he came to the conclusion that perhaps few listeners were persuadable. Before this ultimate moment, there was probably not any significant change over the years either in the positions for which he argued or in his motivation for undertaking the argument. He must have spoken on national issues in Israel count-less dozens of times. I will focus here on two talks he gave in his last year and a half because they constitute, in very different ways, a grand summation of his sense of the political realities and the demographic contexts in which they are embedded.

First, however, I would like to backtrack to 1982, to a book that gives no expression of Amos's political views apart from a single extended passage but that nevertheless provides a win-dow into the matrix of those views. In the fall of 1982, shortly after the first Lebanon war, Amos traveled around the country and engaged in a series of conversations (they were not really interviews) with people whose values and allegiances widely dif-fered from one another's and also from his. Depending on the character of his interlocutors, a couple of these were more mono-logues than conversations. Each locale with its distinctive look and sounds is skillfully evoked with the novelist's experienced touch, but the heart of the book is what the different interlocu-tors say. From time to time, Amos pushes them with questions, but he does not intervene to comment, or to object or interpret. He did not record the conversations but reconstructed them from memory, with impressive fidelity to the kind of Hebrew each spoke, from ostentatious pious to demotic to fiercely rhe-torical. This, we may conclude, constitutes a modest but effec-tive intervention in the book by the novelist exercising his craft. The results of this listening to speakers across the political and social spectrum were published in 1983 under the title *A Jour-ney in the Land of Israel*. I should add that the second term in the Hebrew title, *eretz yisra'el*, sometimes extends to mean "Israel-Palestine." In fact, the conversations include two with Palestin-ians on their turf and another two with West Bank settlers.

Strikingly, Amos chose, with one partial exception, to speak with people whose views were completely unlike his own. In a prefatory note, he says that the conversations are by no means intended to be a representative cross-section of Israel's variegated inhabitants. But here is the instructive sequence of those with whom he spoke: ultra-Orthodox Jews in the general vicinity of his childhood home in Jerusalem; working-class Jews of Middle Eastern background in the development town Beit-Shemesh; Israeli nationalists in the settlement of Tekoa in the West Bank; Palestinians in the city of Ramallah and in the Occupied Territories; a brutally militant Zionist in his rural home; modern Orthodox settlers in the town of Ofra in the West Bank; the Palestinian editor of an Arab-language journal in East Jerusalem; a French monk who was a professor of philosophy at the Hebrew University; a man and wife in their seventies who had spent all their lives as farmers in a small village near Zichron Yaakov, some miles south of Haifa; an older man who came to Israel from Romania and settled in Ashdod, a port city on the Mediterranean founded in 1957.

I present this catalogue of the book's contents in order to convey the extreme variety, despite whatever groups were not included, of the people with whom Amos spoke. It is as though an American writer set out to write *A Journey in America* and met with Christian fundamentalists, inner-city Black people, fervid supporters of Trump, recent Mexican immigrants, and White nationalists, but not with any country-club Republicans, New York intellectuals, or centrist or progressive Democrats.

In the gallery of interlocutors in *A Journey in the Land of Israel*, some do not merely differ in outlook from Amos but hold views that were surely anathema to him. Among the ultra-Orthodox in Jerusalem, he hears two words vehemently repeated, "Messiah" and "Hitler." The Messiah is bound to come sooner or later, but very likely sooner, and it is he who will effect a grand national restoration, not the deluded and overweening *Tzionistin,* as these Orthodox call the Zionists in the Yiddish version of the designation. Whoever fails to recognize this inevitability, whoever impedes its advent, is an heir to Hitler, an active accomplice in his nefarious designs to destroy the Jewish people. Amos hears out these fervent views but does not attempt to debate them, and there surely could have been no possible common ground for discussion. The same is true for entirely different reasons with the two groups of settlers with whom he met, though, exceptionally, at Ofra, he decided to present a limited counterargument toward the end of his brief stay there. Among the Mizrahi workers in Beit-Shemesh, he encountered long-seething resentment against the Ashkenazi ruling class for shunning them, mistreating them, holding them in contempt, keeping all the nation's privileges for themselves. Politically, Beit-Shemesh had embraced Begin (then the prime minister) and his Likud party, even though he himself came from Poland and was a "white" Jew. One cannot debate with resentment, and Amos makes no gesture to do so.

The most shocking conversation in the book is the one with the uncompromisingly aggressive nationalist. His chapter is a virtually uninterrupted monologue, as befits his intransigent views. For him, history is an arena of brutal violence, and the only way to prevail is to be more brutal than all the others: "Let them tremble. Let them call me a crazy country. Let them understand that we are a wild country, a mortal danger to the whole neighborhood, a holy terror, abnormal, prepared to go crazy because they murdered just one kid of ours, to run wild and burn all the oil fields of the Middle East." If it comes to igniting a third world war, he is ready for it. He sums up his attitude: "As long as you're fighting for your very existence, anything is permitted. Even what is forbidden is permitted. Even driving the Arabs out of the West Bank. Anything." Amos cloaks the speaker's identity in anonymity, but the conclusion of many Israeli readers of the book was that it was Ariel Sharon. More than two decades later, Sharon would oversee the unilateral Israeli evacuation of the Gaza Strip. As Amos often remarked, things can change, sometimes unpredictably.

Surprisingly, the interlocutors who express attitudes that in some ways jibe with Amos's are the Palestinians. The young men in Ramallah with whom he spoke—they are wearing jeans and T-shirts with "Coca-Cola" emblazoned on the front—simply want to live and let live. One of them tells him: "Here's the deal with the Jews and Arabs here. It's like two guys on a roof hanging on hard to each other. Either they will fall together from the roof or they will be careful[. . . .] If they go out of control, the two of them will break their heads and their legs." This could serve as a pithy summary of Amos's sense of the conflict. Forty years later, as conditions worsened, he would have been less likely to find anyone in the Occupied Territories talking like this. Another interlocutor, the editor of the Palestinian journal in East Jerusalem, on a higher level of sophistication, is prepared, grudgingly, to accept the necessity that the area should be divided between the two peoples, even if it means that the Palestinians will have to give up the once-Arab towns of Yafo and Acco on the Mediterranean coast. When the book appeared, this editor was attacked by other Palestinians for collaborating with the Zionist enemy, and then he claimed that Amos had tendentiously misrepresented his views.

The older couple in the village near Zichron is the one set of interlocutors not entirely distanced from Amos in either outlook or identity. They are authentic old-style Zionists who have worked the same plot of land all their lives, doing almost everything with their own hands. Morally admirable but also rather moralistic, they vehemently disapprove of almost everything that Israel has become—the materialism, the careerism, the self-indulgence, the aping of America, the abandonment of Zionism's goal of returning to the soil. They would like to see a national program in which everyone would be obliged to devote time to physical labor, preferably in agriculture, from the cabinet ministers and the members of the Knesset to members of the new entrepreneur class. In their talk with Amos, they do not touch on the conflict with the Palestinians. Again, Amos makes no comment, though we can infer that he admires them but sees what they represent as the vestige of a vanished period, vanished not only for the urban population of Israel but also for him and his fellow kibbutzniks.

The author's single rejoinder to his interlocutors in the book occurs during the days he spent at Ofra, the West Bank settlement of modern Orthodox nationalists. It was arranged for him to address a group of them on the Saturday evening of his stay, and he incorporates a summary of his remarks at the end of the two Ofra chapters. Here it becomes clear why he undertook this book and how it offers a key to his enterprise as a political activist. "All the streams of Zionism," he tells his audience, "even those that are alien to me and frighten me, are compelling to me as a storyteller." He goes on to say that he does not view the play of conflicting positions as an amused literary observer but as someone deeply engaged in the issues.

> Even when certain stances drive me crazy, I do not cease being deeply moved by this phenomenon, that people with different intentions and different worldviews basically agree with one another that the Jews need to come home, but they do not agree, and they bitterly struggle with one another, on the plan of the home and its contents. I lovingly accept (for the most part) the mosaic of beliefs and opinions.

On another occasion he underlines the position put forth in these remarks, saying that he loves Israel even when he can't stand it.

This is what *A Journey in the Land of Israel* is all about: his love of Israel. The book also reflects the driving force of his lifelong dedication to political activism. At Ofra, perfectly aware that he will not win over his listeners to his views, convinced as they are that their presence in the West Bank is part of a divine providential plan for the people of Israel, he aims to persuade them of the necessity for a pluralistic orientation toward the disputed national agenda. The bedrock assumption that he feels should bind together all the disparate groups is that the Jews must have a national home, that they cannot dispense with their shared culture and their shared social reality even though those entail the most bitter differences in regard both to political and religious outlook and to the intractable relations with the other populations in the region. The stance of a reasonable pluralist, as Amos knew from experience over the years, was not going to make anyone altogether popular in a country where so many groups and individuals cling to their varying views with fierce intransigence.

In the last pages of the book, Amos refers to letters he has been receiving—his journey antedated e-mail—in which he is denounced as a traitor, a defeatist, a murderer, an heir to Hitler. For many on the Israeli Right, he came to figure as the arch proponent of everything they detested and feared. A Mizrahi taxi driver taking me from Beersheba, when he heard that Ben-Gurion University had just given the award for the best graduating senior in Hebrew literature to an Arab student, said, with an edge of contempt, "Ah, that's Amos Oz again." Anyone preaching moderation, moreover, is bound to get slammed from both sides. Years ago, a radical leftist Israeli professor pronounced to me without qualification, "Amos Oz and Meir Kahana are just the same." Although he did not spell out what he meant by this outrageous equation of an Israeli liberal with a militant racist and violent nationalist, the implication was that if you were a Zionist, if you insisted that the Jews had a right to national autonomy in some part of Israel-Palestine, you belonged to the same pernicious gang as the most murderous nationalists. In his later years, Amos was often the target of resentment from both ends of the political spectrum. He had long been the poster child of liberal Zionism, which was now frequently seen to be in eclipse. Amos accepted that he would be reviled by fiercely uncompromising extremists of the Right and of the Left, yet he remained a staunch advocate of the existential necessity for pluralism in

Israel's national life. *A Journey in the Land of Israel* bears witness to that necessity.

In its closing pages, the book returns briefly to Ashdod, reporting fragments of conversations overheard by the visitor. What the conversations reflect is the sheer, more or less tranquil ordinariness of everyday life in an Israeli town. One woman invites a neighbor to come over that Friday night. They may discuss politics, she says, but they have a video they can watch together. Another mentions her son who is coming back from the army. There is talk of salaries, of a new house under construction. The people on whom Amos eavesdrops in Ashdod differ from him in cultural level and social sensibility, but the point is that they are quite naturally living their day-to-day lives, unconsumed by ideology, paying some attention to politics as one can scarcely avoid doing in this country but not driven or maddened by the political realm, experiencing an underlying sense of ease as Jews in a Jewish-majority state. Amos can comfortably embrace such people: in a way, they are the living rationale for Zionism.

Before turning to the explicit political argument of Amos's addresses to the public, I would like to touch briefly on a late talk that would seem to have nothing to do with politics but that goes to the heart of his allegiance to Zionism. On December 6, 2017, a year before his death, at the Israel Institute for International Studies, Amos gave a talk that he called "Israeli Reflections." His subject was the Hebrew language and what had happened to it in the Zionist revival and in the Hebrew literature on European soil that was a necessary prelude to that revival. He reminds his audience what an altogether unlikely and seemingly quixotic enterprise it was more than a century earlier to write novels and poems in Hebrew and to disseminate Hebrew journals. The publications could have in some cases reached no more than a few hundred readers, perhaps at most one or two thousand, nor did the authors and editors have much hope of actually making a living from their publication. Yet the writers stubbornly persisted. Amos cites the example of the novelist Yosef Haim Brenner, who fled Russia during the first decade of the twentieth century, landing in London, where he edited a Hebrew journal he founded there, contributing many of its articles, even setting type for it with his own hands. At any given point, the circulation of the journal numbered only in the hundreds.

Despite such improbable beginnings, the Hebrew language took root in the Zionist movement in Palestine, and by the 1920s it was well on the way to becoming the spoken language of a few hundred thousand. As Amos observes, a common language became necessary when a Jew from Russia or Poland wanted to communicate with a Jew from Iraq or Yemen, and it was a real language, not just an odd literary project, when a young man from one group wanted to say to a young woman from another group, "I love you." Just a handful of Hebrew readers in Europe around 1900 had become, he says, ten million in Israel a hundred years later. That number probably represents a rhetorical flourish, but even if the number is reduced to a more realistic six or seven million, the growth from humble beginnings is spectacular. As Amos notes, seeking to put this development in perspective, there are far more readers of Hebrew now than readers of Danish, Norwegian, or Finnish, and in Shakespeare's time, there were approximately just two million readers of English.

Amos drives home this point, as he often did in his lectures, with a personal anecdote. When the Oz family was traveling through Italy, they paid a visit in Rome, as most tourists do, to the Coliseum. Outside the impressive Roman structure copies of a brochure about the Coliseum, available in twenty-six languages, were being sold at a stand. One of those languages was Hebrew—Hebrew and not Latin, it dawned on Amos—and he began to cry.

Why did the presence of the one language and the absence

of the other move him in this way, and what does his celebration of the persistence and renaissance of Hebrew have to do with his politics? The obvious reason for his emotional response to the tourist brochure was the contrast between the Coliseum, an imposing if crumbling stone edifice that is the inert vestige of Roman grandeur, and the living Hebrew language, vibrant expression of continuing Jewish life. The language of the Roman conquerors of Judea had long vanished from everyday usage, but the descendants of the conquered people were still very much alive.

Less obvious is the relevance of Hebrew to Amos's politics. In one of his talks, he said that he, though a sworn enemy of every kind of fanaticism, was a fanatic about just one thing: the Hebrew language. In part, this reflects a writer's powerful attachment to the language that is his medium, an attachment that started when as a child he began to discover through Teacher Zelda Hebrew's layered magical richness, something that is scarcely detectable in the Hebrew of the streets. Because Amos's stature as a writer has been widely established through translation, with notably apt translations into English, Italian, and German, his millions of readers abroad can have no real sense of the resonance, both powerful and subtle, of his work in the original and of how meaningful that resonance was for him and continues to be for his Hebrew readers.

But the talk at the Institute for International Studies does not focus on his relation to Hebrew as a writer. Instead it highlights how Hebrew has reflected the stubbornly enduring life of the Jews over the centuries. Amos correctly observes that it was never a dead language but rather, in his apt metaphor, a sleeping beauty, first awakened by the fumbling kiss of the Haskalah, the Hebrew Enlightenment of the nineteenth century, then brought back to full life by Zionism. In invoking the image of a sleeping beauty, he surely meant that Hebrew, even after ceasing to be a vernacular language, continued to be used by

Jews not merely for religious purposes but in community chronicles, international business correspondence, wills, histories, and poetry—some of the greatest poetry produced anywhere in the Middle Ages was written in Hebrew by Jews in Andalusia, though the language that all of the poets were speaking was Arabic. While the Coliseum dropped out of use and gradually decayed, Hebrew added strata, expanded its vocabulary, became an instrument of philosophy, the expression in poetry of personal loss and love, even a medium for laying out in verse the rules of chess, and in all these varying ways it made possible the eventual, spectacular revival that Amos celebrates in his lecture.

What underpins Amos's conception of Jewish national existence in Israel is that the Jews were and remain a people. They were a people before they were a religious group—in fact, "religion" is not an especially relevant term for the biblical worldview—and before they were the adherents of an ideology of nationalism (there are several competing ideologies within the Zionist camp). Every people has a language in which to carry out its daily life and its culture, and Hebrew—even as Jews adopted other languages and in several instances made them distinctively Jewish—continued to have partial awakenings during its long slumber and continued to serve that collective purpose. After its re-establishment in Palestine as a language of everyday life through the early decades of the twentieth century, it became, like languages elsewhere, the natural manifestation of belonging to the same people. Although ideological motives impelled the revivers of Hebrew, the vividly awakened language transcends ideology. Almost everybody in Israel uses it, the settlers, the leftist activists, the young men and women frequenting the cafés and clubs of Tel Aviv, the Arab citizens of Israel, even the ultra-Orthodox despite the continuing ideological attachment of many of them to Yiddish.

Amos's loving devotion to Hebrew and his celebration of the language should be seen in connection with the pluralism that he promotes in *A Journey in the Land of Israel*. He assumes that there are vehement, sometimes even violent differences on many essential issues—on religious observance and the role of religion in national life, on economic policy, on the importance of ethnic identity, and, above all, on what to do about the Occupied Territories. But he would argue that Israelis, as Hebrew speakers, belong to a single people: the vitality of the shared Hebrew language binds them together as a people and could become one enabling condition for setting the nation on a path that would make its endangered future viable. The celebration of Hebrew was thus not only a cultural affirmation for Amos but also a political act. Just as he believed that it was an eminently sound move for Jews to come home to the Land of Israel where, for all their bickering about the character of the home, they were able to enjoy a collective existence, he saw the Hebrew language as the living embodiment of the reality that they belong together as a people despite the acute differences among them. This view of national existence is ultimately hopeful, and Amos's political vision had to be sustained by hope under conditions—particularly political conditions—that could often seem hopeless.

Two explicitly political lectures Amos delivered in Hebrew when he was well into his seventies constitute a lucid and cogent formulation of the position on the conflict for which he had been arguing ever since the end of the Six-Day War and thus can stand in for all the numerous talks he gave on this vexed topic over the years. They also convey a sense of why he felt the need to devote himself to political activism from the time he came of age almost to the very end.

The earlier of these two talks was delivered at the Museum of the Land of Israel in Tel Aviv on February 17, 2015. In an exception to his usual practice, he had a prepared text on the lectern in front of him and read from the text throughout, perhaps because he wanted to make his argument clear and precise, with no essential point left out. But his reading, like his more informal presentation in his other lectures, was forceful and emphatic. In this talk, he made little use of metaphorical language or homey anecdotes and instead pressed hard to lay out the factual argument for a two-state solution to the conflict. A revised version of this talk became one of the three chapters of his short book *Dear Zealot*. By 2015, voices from many sides in Israel and abroad were declaring that it was now too late, that the two-state solution was finished. Even Amos's friend A. B. Yehoshua, always a man of the Left but disposed to espouse quixotic positions on political and historical issues, published an article around this time contending that the only viable option remaining was for the Israelis and the Palestinians to join in a single state where they could learn to live together in amity, and he continued to maintain this view until his death in 2022. The line of defense Amos took up was that this alternative to two states side by side would inevitably prove to be catastrophic, so some way had to be found to rescue the embattled idea, perhaps not now but somewhere down the road.

One state in the territory of Israel-Palestine, he bluntly affirms, would inevitably end up becoming an Arab state. "If we stay in the Territories, there will in the end be an Arab state from the Jordan to the sea." Here is why: given birth rates and demography, the majority of the population would be Palestinian before long. At that point, the country would already be a de facto Arab state, or the Jewish minority would be constrained to govern it as a dictatorship. As he soberly notes, the fate of all such ethnic or religious dictatorships imposed on a majority ethnic or religious group is to be overthrown. The notion, moreover, that the two peoples in such a state would equally coexist flies in the face of the evidence of history: not a single state in the Arab world has minorities that are not discriminated against, persecuted, or worse. In this one-state scenario, then, the Jewish population of present-day Israel would become a subjugated people, as they had been so often in the Diaspora, and large numbers of them, it could be reasonably assumed, would be impelled to flee. Amos also reminds his audience, as he did in many other lectures, that multiethnic or multireligious states elsewhere, with the sole exception of Switzerland, have ended badly, in bloodbaths, as happened in Lebanon, Cyprus, Northern Ireland, and elsewhere.

Then he addresses the issue of a military solution. The formidable armed forces of Israel have, with good reason, generally given its citizens a sense of security; many in the country feel that a strong military presence in the West Bank and along the borders is a reassuring safeguard against terrorism and invasion. But to think that security is gained through arms, Amos tells his audience, is a dangerous illusion. The Israeli army can avert disaster in the short term, but it "cannot achieve any goal." "After 1967," he argues, "we have never won a war." This is hardly a proposition many Israelis would like to hear, but the evidence supports his contention. It is by no means clear that Israel really "won" the 1973 war or the two incursions into Lebanon. The attacks against the Gaza Strip, which some Israelis, in a dubious metaphor, refer to as "mowing the grass," have only reinforced the determination of Hamas, which in each round deploys more advanced weapons toward its stated goal of wiping the State of Israel off the map.

Amos reminds his audience of the global context of the local conflict. The Israeli Right is predisposed to dismiss world opinion, but Amos argues that isolation by the international community would have dire consequences for the Jewish state and that "we are already halfway to being boycotted by the world." Geostrategically, in light of the technological development of weaponry, all of Israel is exposed to Arab missiles; even beyond the Middle East, Israel is open to actual or potential missiles from Islamic states such as Pakistan and Indonesia. Most ominously, nuclear weapons will inevitably proliferate among hostile nations. Amos's summary of this situation is blunt, as is everything else in this talk: "We were always weaker than our enemies."

Amos forcefully offers a critical analysis of the commonly held position on both sides of the conflict in order to frame the validity of each group's claim to the land. A "right," he proposes, "is not what I want but what is recognized by others." Thus the Palestinian claim to every square inch from the Jordan to the sea has no grounding in general opinion except on the anti-Zionist international Left; and the Israeli settlers' claim of a right to the whole West Bank and even, for some, to the Temple Mount is no more than a dangerous partisan assertion. Amos summarizes the bedrock principle of his understanding of the conflict in a single short sentence: "We are not alone in this land." On the Palestinian side (not dealt with in this address to fellow Israelis) many no doubt prefer to think that at least in principle they are alone in this land, but the implied corollary of Amos's argument is that in the end circumstances will compel them to recognize that they are not alone. Throughout the talk, Amos firmly acknowledges the bitterness of the long enmity between Arabs and Jews, and in fact he views their vying claims to the land as a powerful argument against the viability of the single-state solution. Jews and Arabs in Israel-Palestine, he reminds his audience, have undergone a hundred years of hatred and bloodshed, which makes it inconceivable that they could live together in amity in a single nation. (As any Israeli would be keenly aware, the violent conflict between Jews and Arabs did not begin after the U.N. partition decision in 1947 but goes back at least to 1921, when the first widespread Arab attacks on the Zionists occurred.) What remains, then, however unlikely its imminent implementation, is the establishment of an independent Palestinian state alongside Israel, with some sort of compromise worked out for East Jerusalem and perhaps, in the distant future, even a federation with the State of Israel.

The details of this lecture on the conflict demonstrate something important about the nature of Amos's political activism. Many would regard him as a pollyannaish liberal, still promoting a two-state solution in the second decade of this century when it had become clear that there was no way to achieve it. The argument, however, of his 2015 lecture and its very language are grounded in hardheaded realism. I think that is why he avoids the rhetorical flourishes and figurative language at which he was so adept: he repeatedly puts things baldly, aiming to make his listeners see the plain, difficult facts: "We are not alone in this land." Through all his years on the political stage, he clung to the idea of a separate existence of Israel alongside a Palestinian state not because he was a starry-eyed optimist but because he recognized that the alternatives were too terrible. Although the electoral realities of Israel may cast doubt on his stubborn optimism for the long range, he clearly needed to hold fast to it, and the optimism, however unwarranted it may seem, is not foolish.

In addition to the realism, another major aspect of Amos's politics emerges in this late lecture. Though the most obvious label for his political outlook would be "liberal," a better way of putting it is to call his politics "humanistic." I do not mean to propose a sentimental encomium but simply to say that he believed any acceptable politics had to place a supreme value on human life. In the little book on fanaticism, he argues that the hallmark of fanatics is that they are so convinced of the absolute rightness of their cause that they are prepared to shed rivers of blood to implement it: if they can't convert you to their cause, which they see as your only path to redemption, they may be obliged to wipe you off the face of the earth so that your recalcitrant presence does not get in the way of the one and only redemption that must inevitably come. Against fanaticism—of all kinds, from nationalism and religion to militant veganism— Amos argues that "democracy and pluralism are, finally, popular expressions of the sanctity of life, of the equality of every human being's value, of [the Talmudic dictum] 'Whoever saves a single person is considered as if he saved the whole world.'" An important corollary of this humanistic politics is a repeated emphasis on the indispensable autonomy of the individual. Again, in Amos's argument with fanaticism, he proposes that fanatics, because they know there is one right way, must submerge their individuality in the mass of those walking in the right way, who all merge into a single collective self. We are each of us, in his view, different from one another, and respect for those differences, and an abiding curiosity about the differences, is necessary for a viable politics. That acceptance of difference is what underlies his argument for pluralism in the talk to the settlers at Ofra.

On June 3, 2018, half a year before his death, Amos gave a lecture at Tel Aviv University. (It can be watched in Hebrew, with subtitles, on YouTube.) It was published in Hebrew after his decease in a slim booklet entitled *The Last Lecture: The Whole Reckoning Is Not Over Yet*. The second half of the title is a quotation from a novel by Yosef Haim Brenner, an unsparingly critical Zionist observer of Zionism and of the Jews who was killed in the Arab assault on the Jewish population of Palestine in 1921. This talk took place more than a year and a half after I had last seen Amos in San Francisco, and he was even more drastically weakened by the advance of the disease and by the continuing chemotherapy. Most people in his condition would surely have declined any lecture invitation, but he, I have to conclude, felt an overriding obligation to speak on the life-and-death issue of the Israelis' conflict with the Palestinians one last time. I think he wanted to present a final summing up of the case he had been making for the two-state solution ever since the early months after the 1967 war. Understandably, he looked gaunt and physically diminished, but when he began to speak, he was energetic and forceful, as he always had been in his lectures.

There was a prepared text in front of him, but unlike in his 2015 talk, he did not read from it, only glanced down at it from time to time.

He began with a modest declaration, "I don't have a lot to say to you this evening," but what he went on to say was an intense synthesis of his stance as a political activist through fifty-one years. In this final presentation, he deploys a couple of metaphors as well as one striking personal anecdote. I have no way of knowing what the political predispositions of that audience were, but even if we reasonably assume that the attendees were largely on the Left, by that late moment many, across the political spectrum, had given up on the two-state solution. Amos, then, did not want merely to lay out the facts of the ongoing conflict, as he had done in 2015, but to win over the audience emotionally to his view, and he adopted a rhetorical strategy appropriate to that end.

The lecture thus begins with a metaphor. The conflict between the Israelis and the Palestinians is "a bleeding infected wound." He extends that metaphor to what it implies about a solution: "You don't cure a wound with a stick." Amos, though an advocate of peace, was by no means a pacifist, and he makes that clear at the beginning of his presentation: "We're here because we had a big stick." The implication would not have been lost on an Israeli audience, keenly aware that in 1948–1949, if the Jews then living in Palestine had not possessed a big stick—fashioned out of a rather little stick—they would all have been destroyed or driven out. Like the brutal nationalist whose words he reported in *A Journey in the Land of Israel*, Amos recognized that the play of competing forces in the world where we live is a hardball game. In a lecture he gave in Berkeley many years earlier, he trotted out a rhetorical set piece that he must have used often. Before Israel, he declared, there was a Jewish polity that was in some regards much more impressive. It spread over a large geographical region in eastern Europe, had its own vibrant language, Yiddish, its institutions of self-governance, its social welfare agencies, a lively press, a rich literature, a theater that could be reckoned among the best in Europe. It lacked, however, a few armored divisions, an air force, and perhaps a little atomic bomb or two, and as a result it was utterly destroyed and millions of its citizens were murdered.

In the last lecture, then, he argues that political autonomy along with the apparatus of power it confers is a necessary condition for the survival of the Jewish people. "I don't want to be a minority!" he declares, with the dire record of the past in mind, "not even in Switzerland, and especially not in an Arab state." As a corollary to this awareness of the painful challenges of national existence, he notes a troubling asymmetry in Israeli and Palestinian views. On the Israeli side, a substantial group, however politically marginalized, recognize the Palestinian need for national autonomy on a territorial base. The Palestinians, on their part, have been fighting "to be a free people in its own land" while denying that same right to the Israelis. Thus, he proposes, the Palestinians have fought two wars, one admirably just and the other unjust. Implicit in their denial of any justice on the other side is a perception of the Israelis as interlopers who simply do not belong. Although Amos does not spell it out in the lecture, he would surely have assumed that any resolution of the conflict will come about only when the force of circumstances compels the Palestinians to alter that perception and accept, however painfully, the reality that there are two peoples, each with the right to its own land.

At this point, Amos undertakes an argument that applies both to the Palestinians and to the Israelis, and he does this through a personal anecdote. On one of his trips to Europe, he met a Palestinian who had been living abroad most of his life. "I'm from Lifta," he told Amos. Lifta is a once-Arab town less than a mile from the Jerusalem neighborhood in which Amos grew up. What the expatriate Palestinian insists on, the desire for "my home in Lifta," is uncompromising—and perhaps also plaintive. Amos's rejoinder is that the Lifta he remembers—though he probably has no actual memories of it—no longer exists and can never exist again. In 1948 it was a peaceful little community of perhaps a thousand people. Now, as a town of twenty thousand or more with high-rise buildings, shopping centers, and the like, it would be totally unrecognizable. Amos's stark conclusion is, "You cannot recover in space what is lost in time." He tells his Palestinian interlocutor, "You are stricken with the disease of *shakhzeret*," using a Hebrew term he has coined that he translates into English as "reconstitutitis." "It is a disease that will drive you crazy."

As a Zionist, Amos is obliged to consider for the sake of his audience whether Zionism as a movement is a pathological manifestation of *shakhzeret* based on the dream of returning to a land that was lost two thousand years earlier. There was, Amos concedes, a certain element of *shakhzeret* in Zionism, but it was essentially confined to anthems and speeches (and, I may add, to a certain trend in poetry). Yet the essential force that drove the Zionist movement, he argues, was persecution: European Jews, and later Middle Eastern Jews, came to Palestine because they had no place else to go. In Germany the Jews were hated because they resembled other Germans too closely; in Poland, because they were too different. In this connection, Amos invokes his paternal grandfather, whose story he told in *A Tale of Love and Darkness*. The grandfather had to flee Russia, and though ideologically a Zionist, he sought an entry visa in one country after another. All rejected his request. Having nowhere else to go, he ended up in Jerusalem, a reluctant immigrant.

Amos then turns to his contention that *shakhzeret* drives you crazy, and considers a group of Israelis who would like to build a third temple in Jerusalem. (Since this would have to be on the Temple Mount, it would entail razing the Al Aksa mosque and thus ignite a war with global Islam.) But, he proposes to his audience, think about the practical side of reconstituting the ancient temple in the twenty-first century. In Israel, with a Jewish population perhaps eight times that of Judea two thousand years ago, a million and a half pilgrims would throng to the temple for the festivals. Where would you house them? How could you provide parking space? What about sanitary facilities? The grand restoration of the temple would rapidly turn into a nightmare: what has been lost in time cannot be found in space. Those who long for the remembered glories of the ancient temple, he concludes, will do better to recover it in poetry, in music, in liturgy.

Given how intractable the conflict is, what hope can there be? To the end Amos clung to the possibility of a solution—it is what kept him going in his activism. He had come to much the same conclusion that the protagonist of Italo Svevo's *The Confessions of Zeno* comes to: "Life is neither good nor bad. It is surprising." This affirmation by Zeno jibes with the one Amos puts forth toward the end of his lecture: "Man is unpredictable." As a political case in point, he cites the meeting in Jerusalem between Anwar Sadat, the architect of the almost successful 1973 Egyptian attack on Israeli forces, and Menachem Begin, the militant Israeli nationalist. Any prediction of a reconciliation in which an Arab head of state flew to Israel and diplomatic relations soon followed would have been regarded not long before it happened as a wild fantasy. It is Amos's contention that, for all the fierce opposition on the Right to the creation of a Palestinian state, the majority of Israelis know in their hearts that sooner or later that state will emerge. He cites as evidence the statistic that 90 percent of Israelis have not set foot in the Occupied Territories for years. Nothing is irreversible, he argues, "only death." To which he adds a wry personal note: "I will soon check that out."

If, in fact, despite the large number of stubborn votes to the contrary, most Israelis know deep down that there is no alternative to the two-state solution, how can that supposed knowledge be implemented as policy? Amos had to cling to hope in order to sustain his role as political activist. At the end of this last lecture, he articulates what a true leader should be by citing something Harry Truman once said. Truman dismissed the notion that the person sitting in the Oval Office was by virtue of his position the most powerful man in the world. Leadership, Truman proposed, should "convince people to do what they know down deep in their hearts they must do." With Benjamin Netanyahu forced out of office as prime minister but then returned to power, it is by no means evident that such a leader is on the horizon, and that was certainly the case in 2018 when Amos spoke these words. Nevertheless, human beings and therefore the course of events are unpredictable, and he needed to cling to hope for the future as he knew his own end was imminent.

Over the years, Amos devoted countless hours and great stores of energy to public advocacy for the cause of peace with the Palestinians. Beyond his appearances for lectures, he was constantly writing opinion pieces in the Hebrew press, sometimes, by his own account, as I have noted, one or even two a week. It was his most engrossing activity after writing fiction. Late in life, he told Shira Hadad that his passionate desire to produce such pieces had waned. He also observed to her that among living Israeli writers, he, A. B. Yehoshua, and David Grossman were "dinosaurs" and that the succeeding generation of novelists and poets did not share their drive to address urgent political questions in public forums.

Did his political efforts have any perceptible impact? In his conversation with Shira Hadad, he appears to be a little skeptical that they did, for, after all, he was a realist. Yet his conscience compelled him to engage in the enterprise of public advocacy for a two-state solution, so he had no choice but to engage, for his conscience, unlike that of many writers in the West, was entwined with the fate of the nation. And in this conversation with Shira Hadad, as at the end of his last lecture, he offers grounds for optimism, without necessarily assuming that his own activity had done anything to prepare those grounds. In 1967, he tells her hyperbolically, you could have held a national conference in a telephone booth for all the supporters of a Palestinian state alongside the State of Israel, but now there were a few million supporters. As a stubborn optimist, he says he looks to the future and to those who will come after him, recalling for Shira Hadad words he had spoken at the funeral of Yosi Sarid, a member of the Knesset and a prominent figure of the Israeli Left. The words could serve as an apt epilogue to his long battle on behalf of a political cause that he felt was vital to the survival of his country as a democratic Jewish state.

> It is not for us to complete the task. Men and women younger
> than we are will come. A new generation will come of people
> who stand for peace and social justice, and this generation
> will perhaps have a different language and different ways of
> debating and different motives from ours. They will perhaps
> find a way to the hearts of the millions of Israelis who until
> now have not agreed with us. Not because they are all racists
> and not because they are all swimming in hatred and brain-
> washed, absolutely not, but because many of them are really
> worried and really fearful, but they may be open to different
> voices from mine and to other motives. Perhaps.

It is safe to assume that many writers would like to leave a legacy. In the end, Amos Oz may have been more concerned with his legacy as a spokesman for peace and reconciliation than as a writer of fiction. He recognized that the generation to come after him would have to be different from him—with a different worldview, a different way of speaking—but the very prospect of differences provided him with a glimmer of hope that they would find a way to change things as he and his contemporaries had not been able to do. However, the ringing affirmation recorded by Shira Hadad concludes with a plaintive single word: perhaps. It expresses the kind of person he was—an inveterate optimist and also an open-eyed realist.

6

Taking Stock

As Amos Oz was turning sixty, indications in his work suggest that he had begun looking back on his life: pondering the wound he had carried since childhood, reflecting on what he had achieved and perhaps also failed to achieve in his writing, and musing over what was by then becoming of his sexuality. Many may experience this impulse to introspection at this point in their lives—sixty is no longer the threshold to old age it once was—but in your sixties you cannot quite think of yourself as young any more, or perhaps even as middle-aged, with the biblical mortality marker of three score and ten looming ahead of you. Thoughts about his sexuality would have beset Amos because it was a significant part of who he was—which may lend some credence to the rumors about affairs. The magnetically attractive young man was now weathered-looking, his face bearing signs of aging after years of exposure to the Middle Eastern sun even as it retained vestiges of handsomeness.

When Amos was sixty-three, he made a personally pivotal decision by at last writing about his mother's suicide in *A Tale of Love and Darkness*. It has often been remarked that he had long cloaked the topic in silence, but that is not entirely accurate, for, as a number of critics have noted, he invoked that traumatic event explicitly, though only in a couple of brief passages, in *The Same Sea*, the experimental novel in verse that had appeared three years earlier. The form of that novel is a reflection of its deeply personal meaning for him. As we have seen, his earliest literary aspirations, from childhood to late adolescence, were to write poetry. His initial collection of short stories was densely lyric, a mode of writing he came to regard as rather misconceived, concluding that a more chastened kind of prose was required for fiction. In *The Same Sea* he produced a novel patently written in verse. Some of it is clearly, evocatively, poetry, with even an occasional deployment of rhyme, though other passages, laid out typographically in long lines of verse, read more like prose. There is a discernible novelistic plot, but the vehicle of poetry is crucial for him as a writer because in this book he wanted to express his sense of his own life as a lyric poet might do it. In the inscription of the copy he sent me, he wrote: "This is the most intimate book I have written." Before commenting on how *The Same Sea* is autobiographical, let me convey a sense of what happens in the book.

The protagonist is a Bulgarian Jew named Albert Danon—his first name is pronounced without sounding the final "t," as in French—recently widowed, living in Bat Yam, a town a little south of Tel Aviv. He has the prosaic profession of tax advisor, but as someone who sits at a desk poring over columns of figures, he may be a wry transmogrification of the author, who pores over words. The recent death of his wife, Nadia, hauntingly expressed at the beginning of the book, is presided over by birdsong, which brings back to her mind as she is dying her idyllic girlhood in Crete. Amos will go on to invent a different birdsong to preside over his mother's death. Here is an illustrative stanza of poetry that calls forth the setting and the mood:

> In Bat Yam days and hot summer mornings
> but evening descends in those mountains. A low fog
> crawls through the crevices. A sharp wind
> howls as though alive and the fading light
> is more and more like a bad dream.

Albert's son, Riko, has gone off to Southeast Asia, where many young Israelis were wandering in pursuit of new experience and perhaps self-discovery. The poems intermittently pick up the far-off Riko, sometimes in narrative report, sometimes in his letters to his father. The two share certain moments of existential reflection. But Albert remains the center of the narrative. The chief complication of the story is that Riko's girlfriend, Dita, displaced from her own quarters, has come to stay with Albert.

Amos has set two different autobiographical figures in this novel, one directly reflecting his own life and the other emphatically transformed. The direct figure makes occasional appearances and is referred to as "the fictional narrator," *hamesaper habadui*. Despite this gesture of fictionality, there is little distance between him and Amos Oz:

> Now that his children have grown up and he has the joy of grandchildren and he's written some books and traveled and spoken and been photographed, now all of a sudden would he go back to writing poetry? As in the bad days of his youth when he would flee to be by himself at the far end of the kibbutz in the reading room, where he would fill page after page with the wail of the jackal? A moody edgy kid with acne, insulted but exercising in the face of it resigned restraint, over and over, sometimes speaking grand phrases, arousing some

mockery and some pity, a beggar at the doors of the girls—
maybe Gila or Tzila would like him to read them a poem he
had just written. Naively imagining that a woman is won with
a sermon or a poem.

These are the words of the fictional narrator, but they are
a transparent transcription of the experience of Amos Oz at
Hulda at the age of fifteen or sixteen. At a couple of points in
the novel, Riko, on the other side of the world, merges with the
father, and Albert connects with the narrator from time to time.
Thus Riko in a short poem ponders a verse from Job that Amos
would cling to in his late conversations with Shira Hadad and
to which Riko gives a decidedly oedipal twist:

> There's another choice verse in Job he quotes to me so I'll
> remember that property and possessions are not the point:

> Naked I came out from my mother's womb
> and naked will I return there: why the race to hoard and
>   store up
> illusory acquisitions. My father is blind
> to the secret hidden in this verse: her womb
> awaits me. I came out. I will return. The cross on the way
> is less important.

And Dita, addressing the narrator, explicitly introduces Amos
Oz's early loss.

> Your mother did away with herself and left you pretty
> crushed[. . . .] Parents who abandon you, it's different, bleeds
> longer. And your mother and her only son. But for how long?
> Your whole life? In my opinion to sit shiva for your mother
> for forty-five years is pretty ridiculous. Not just ridiculous.
> An insult to other women. To your wife. And to the daugh-
> ters. [. . .] Get up on your hind legs and finally throw her away.
> Exactly as she did to you. Let her wander through her forests
> through the nights but without you. Let her find herself an-
> other sucker.

The mother here is not a fiction but Fania Klausner, complete with her tales of dark forests, and her son is Amos. But putting these angry words in the mouth of a fictional character enables the writer to express the rage pent up within him for so many years. In his next book, he would seek catharsis in novelistically imagining his mother's suicide almost moment by moment, but, as we shall see, the pain lingered after the writing. Here, the anger is directed not only toward his mother but also toward himself—for mourning, sitting shiva, for not letting go of the suicide after so many years (forty-five would be roughly the number of years after his mother's death to the moment when he was first drafting this novel). And for Dita to cast the self-inflicted death as an abandonment was precisely how Amos habitually saw it till the very end, leading him, all his life, to fear being abandoned and to recoil from abandoning others.

Beyond the death of the mother, the novel is punctuated by broodings over the death that inevitably awaits everyone. Thoughts of a lonely death plague Riko, who presumably is a young man in his twenties:

> In fact, everyone is condemned to wait for his death in a separate cage. You, too, your wandering, your obsession with traveling far and gathering experiences, drag your cage with you to the end of the zoo. Each person and his imprisonment. A meshwork screen separates everyone from everyone.

A related passage, which should probably be attributed to Riko but could conceivably be assigned to Albert, flaunts the pointedly distorted citation of Scripture that is a frequent stylistic characteristic of these poems.

> Sweet is the light to the eyes. Darkness sees with the heart. The cord goes after the bucket. In the well, the pitcher is lost. The humble moshavnik who never in his life has sat in the session of scoffers, will die in August from pancreatic cancer.

The policeman who cried wolf will die in September from heart failure. His eyes are sweet and the light is sweet but his eyes are no more and the light is still here. The session of scoffers has closed down instead, and a shopping center has opened. The scoffers have passed away, diabetes, kidneys. Happy is the well, happy the bucket. Happy the humble of spirit, for to them shall surely come the wolf, the wolf.

Amos was a secular person, at times assertively secular, but as is still true for many Hebrew writers, countless verses from the Bible swarmed through his head, addressing him, making him wonder whether they might be saying something relevant to his world or had to be turned around, aggressively rejected. "Sweet is the light to the eyes" is a direct quotation from Ecclesiastes 11:17, one of the few affirmations of life in that book. "Darkness sees with the heart" is an emphatic reversal of 1 Samuel 16:7: "For not as man sees does God see. For man sees with the eyes and the Lord sees with the heart." In this death-haunted book, it is darkness, not God, that exercises penetrating vision. "The cord goes after the bucket" is a Hebrew proverb with the sense that one thing is a necessary consequence of another. The language then returns to the Bible in an untranslatable wordplay: a moshavnik is someone who lives in a moshav, a cooperative village, but here the word leads the writer to a phrase in the first verse of Psalms, "nor in the session of scoffers [*moshav letsim*] has sat." In that psalm, the wicked perish and the righteous flourish. Here, all perish from one disease or another. The poem worries away at the phrases quoted at the beginning—the session of scoffers, the sweet light, the bucket in the well, and crying wolf—the wolf in the end will devour us all. This brief poem is an example of how the poetry of the book makes the Bible an existential sounding board as it turns it inside out. Mortality is clearly a subject on which Amos was brooding as he turned sixty.

Later in the book, a poem pointedly entitled *Stabat Mater*, after the hymn to the suffering mother of Jesus, expresses Riko's gloomy thoughts. They are gloomy because he recently lost his mother, and they converge with the thoughts of the narrator-author.

> To the four corners. Dust of abandonment. My mother. Dust of unfelt extinction. Ash of forgotten houses that have collapsed. Windswept quicksand. Earth going back to earth: from a handful of cosmic dust this planet crystallized, and to a black maw it returns.

As elsewhere, the death of the mother—Riko's, Amos's—is seen as an abandonment, and it interfuses with extinction, collapse, crumbling to dust and ashes, the black maw that will swallow up all things, even the planet we inhabit.

In this most intimate of all Amos's novels, undertaken as he was crossing into his sixties, the author ponders the death of his mother and mortality itself, the decay and death of all things. In tandem with these bleak reflections are thoughts that touch on aging and the slow receding of sexual fulfillment. In this regard, Albert, as different as he is culturally, ethnically, and vocationally from his creator, is partly an autobiographical figure, just as Riko sometimes voices the author's thoughts, while, much more explicitly, the "fictional narrator" is autobiographical. Albert, too, is on the verge of his sixties. As a widower, which Amos never became, he embodies the condition of loneliness that is one of the preoccupations of this book. Deprived of the woman who had been his lover for many years, he is now in the potentially precarious situation of sharing his home with his son's attractive girlfriend. Although he is clearly attracted to her, he is a decent person and will in no way permit himself to make any overture that would compromise his role as fatherly host. Thus, having invited her to move into Riko's vacant room, he is explaining where she will find whatever she needs, but he stops short in his explanation because she has just emerged from the shower wrapped in a towel: "For within the towel her hips are breathing / and he blushes as though exposed in his wicked intention." This is not at all a literally autobiographical moment, but it originates in a man who once had before him a world of alluring young women and now senses the ineluctable process of aging and fears that world is beginning to recede.

Amos, as becomes even clearer in some of the thoughts he shared with Shira Hadad toward the end of his life, had a heavily fraught vision of women as objects of desire. In his view, they held within them the promise of magical pleasure but seemed elusive—at times unattainable—triggers of perhaps inadmissible impulses in the male; they are always mysterious and, as he says elsewhere, the ones who have the power—"to grant their favors" if they so choose—he uses the Hebrew equivalent for the antiquated English expression. Here are Albert's most revealing thoughts on women and desire: "Woman is a pot overflowing with honey and shame, a locked garden, a garden of well-hidden lust till the coming of her redeemer, the evil eye of her redeemer, who disgusts her; no alien male shall draw near but also shall not go far off; starve him, keep him thirsty, but from time to time grant him a crumb, always carefully, as though in perfect innocence, lest you become a mockery and disgrace." The "locked garden" is a phrase from the Song of Songs, but nothing could be further from the Song's exuberant celebration of eros than Albert's thoughts.

This perception of woman, which is surely Amos's as well as Albert's, imagines her as an enticing, beckoning treasure of delight but also barely attainable, imperious, the one who commands the gates to sexual gratification and who somehow is also associated with feelings of shame. In *What's in an Apple?*, a set of intimate revelations recorded by Shira Hadad, a chapter is devoted to his thoughts about women and sexuality. The connection between them and Albert's troubled reflections is unmistakable. Woman, as Amos speaks about her, is a lodestone of desire that is ultimately ungraspable by the limited imagination of the male: "Woman's sexuality," he says in this late conversation, "is in my eyes incomparably richer and more complex than man's sexuality. The difference between a man's sexuality and a woman's is perhaps something like the difference between a drum and a violin." Shira Hadad, several decades his junior and, like many young women, a feminist, tries to push back on such views, but he scarcely budges. This mystification of woman, the attribution to her of unfathomable power, is not a notion that is now likely to sit comfortably with many people. I will not presume to propose any psychoanalytic explanation, but it can certainly be linked to certain way stations in his life story, some of which he tells in *A Tale of Love and Darkness* and more in what he tells Shira Hadad.

By his own account, growing up in Jerusalem left him in complete ignorance of girls; his only notion of sex was gleaned from furtive glances at crude pornographic images: "I was a total erotic illiterate. I was a Neanderthal in everything related to girls." Then came the shock of the transition to Hulda at the post-puberty age of fourteen and a half: "After the raging hormonal hell of Takhemoni [his Orthodox grammar school], I awoke one morning in Hulda. Listen, to move all of a sudden from that monastic Jerusalem to a kind of oasis of permissiveness, it was an emotional and sexual shock the like of which I had never experienced." He adds to this, amusingly, "During my first days on the kibbutz it seemed to me that I was a Muslim suicide bomber, a *shahid*, who arrives in paradise and discovers the seventy-two promised beauties." Just a bit later in this conversation, he offers a different comical comparison: "At Hulda I was like a yeshiva student awakening in a striptease club." Amos's reaction notwithstanding, the kibbutz was hardly a bourn of sensuality. The shorts then worn by the girls, fitting tight up to the crotch, as he recalls, were not meant to be sexy but utilitarian: clothing on the kibbutz disregarded traditional femininity. To

Amos, however, coming from repressed Jerusalem, those completely exposed thighs constituted a flashpoint of lust.

The seventy-two lovely virgins were inaccessible to him. He was the pale, unathletic outsider, the denizen of "monastic" Jerusalem, with no way to approach the girls except through the preposterous medium of his melancholy poems. Then, at sixteen, came his sexual initiation by his teacher Orna, a woman twice his age, who took the initiative when she detected the bulging evidence of his adolescent desire. She was kind and sexually welcoming and showed him what he needed to do, but after they had finished, she told him, quite understandably, that they could not repeat what they had done. Orna had "granted him her favors" and then firmly withdrawn them for the future. We can readily see how the young Amos, desperately deprived ever since the onset of puberty, then rapturously gratified, then deprived once again, should have developed an abiding sense of woman as alluring, powerful, and in some ultimate way sexually inscrutable. This experience is surely the source of the enigmatic, vividly imagined Atalia in *Judas*, and the character of Shmuel Asch is a stand-in, at least sexually, for the author when he was an adolescent.

Amos was by no means entirely stuck with this early tormented longing for woman as an unattainable object of desire. Toward the end of this conversation with Shira Hadad about sex, he also tells her that the physical and emotional fusion of two bodies, two people, is a transcendent experience. She comments that, banal as it may seem, his vision of the erotic is very close to love. He responds: "It's not at all banal, what you said. There are all kinds of levels of the erotic in the world, all kinds of alleys and all kinds of passageways, avenues and one-way streets, and also traps. But the best place in all the great city of the erotic is love." She says he is a romantic, and he agrees, confessing that what he has just talked about is something he has actually experienced. In the end, the evolution of his own sexuality from the pangs of adolescent floundering to love enabled him to represent this realm in his novels through a broad range of its sundry inflections, from the torments of frustration to the impulses of self-destruction to something that might be called love.

In the course of the free-ranging conversations with Shira Hadad, as Amos recounts the difficult transition from Hulda to Arad he comes to say that he should have left the kibbutz much earlier, well before his son Daniel's asthma compelled him to leave. Though he never abandoned his commitment to the socialist ideal, he expresses guilt over having stayed on the kibbutz as long as he did. He notes, without explanation, that it was not good for Nily to be there. But the more acute issue was the children's house, which he thinks seriously harmed his two daughters. The institution of separate children's quarters had begun not out of an ideological principle but out of practical necessity. In the rudimentary material conditions of the early kibbutzim, the adults slept in tents, and an actual house was built only for the children. An ideological rationale was developed after the fact: the children, freed from the negative influences of their parents, who had grown up in the bourgeois framework of the nuclear family, would develop as healthy, well-adjusted members of the new egalitarian community. The reality, Amos says, was quite the opposite. He describes the children's house in shocking terms: "At night after the grownups said goodnight and went off, the children's house sometimes turned into the desert island of *Lord of the Flies*. Woe to the weak ones. Woe to the sensitive ones. Woe to the oddballs. It's a cruel place. I am ashamed that I allowed my children to grow up in children's houses on the kibbutz." In saying this he is clearly not only thinking about what happened to Fania and Galia but also remembering his own experience, when he was flung at the age of fourteen and a half from the claustral apartment where he grew up into the children's house, where he was, exactly, a weak, sensitive, poetry-writing oddball.

Beyond these conversations, there is literary evidence that late in life Amos was troubled by painful thoughts about all those years he spent on the kibbutz, first as a lonely teenager and then with his family. *Between Friends* (2012), his last book of stories, throws a very different light than *Where the Jackals Howl* does on the sad fates of many souls in what was meant to become a socialist utopia. In that first volume of stories, it was, for the most part, traits of individual character that led to loneliness, unhappiness, despair, or even self-destruction. In *Between Friends* the institutions of the kibbutz are chiefly at fault. One wrenching story, "A Little Child," actually represents the children's house as something out of *Lord of the Flies:* a weak, sickly five-year-old boy, who endures the humiliation of being a chronic bed-wetter, is set upon by the other children after the lights go out and the adult responsible for the house leaves, and they gleefully tear apart the rubber duck to which he constantly clings. In another story, a sensitive adolescent is made acutely uncomfortable by the uncompromising insistence of his class teacher that the coming revolution can be carried out only through ruthlessness, to which all must be committed.

Amos, repeatedly reflecting on fanaticism as time went on, shows in these stories that socialist utopianism can generate its own variety of fanaticism, denying individual needs, demanding conformity. In the concluding story, "Esperanto," a kibbutz member dying of emphysema never swerves from his faith that this invented language will unite all the peoples of the world. He resolutely announces, "People are essentially good and generous and decent, and it's only the environment that corrupts them," to which a woman friend who cares about him responds, "But what is the environment? After all, more people." In the end, Amos did not categorically dismiss the kibbutz as an ideological delusion. He saw something admirable, even necessary, in the egalitarian aspirations on which the kibbutz movement was built, but he also felt it was founded on an unrealistic idea of human nature. After all, as a novelist he was an observer of human nature in all its contradictions, its perversities, its persistent ambiguities, and in the human need for independence.

Beyond these thoughts about ideology and social realities, Amos Oz's last years led him to certain unflinching perceptions about himself. Not much more than four years passed from the initial diagnosis of cancer to his death. As anyone knows who has been close to someone similarly afflicted, the dire process goes through predictable stages: after the diagnosis, the punishing course of chemotherapy with the patient hoping the treatment might eradicate the disease; then a remission, leaving the person still in hope; then a recurrence, during which a renewed course of chemotherapy begins to feel like hostile torment, with the patient now struggling with the awareness that the end is near. As Samuel Johnson said, the prospect of an imminent hanging concentrates the mind. Such concentration is perceptible in the two published late-life sets of conversations, the one recorded by Shira Hadad and the other, which incorporates some recorded passages of Amos's thoughts, by Nurith Gertz.

Amos said one rather startling thing to Nurith about himself in those final months, which she reports at the beginning of her book. It is worth quoting and pondering. As is clear, he was aware that in one way or another she intended to write about their conversations, and he framed some of what he told her accordingly. "And don't write just good things about me," he told her. "Also write, 'This was a spoiled guy.' Also write, 'This was a guy chasing honors.' Also write, 'This was a guy too much in love with hearing himself.'" To which she responds, "And I'll also write that this was a guy who was hard to dig into and [it was hard] to know what beneath the disguises and the images was real." Amos embraces this remark and expands on it:

> That, too, you should write. Write that this guy was a walking masquerade ball. That he tried so hard to please them all,

how much he tried to please people who did not even deserve to be pleased, write it all. Don't write a poetic encomium, don't write a love poem, that's not what I need. Write for Nily, for Fania, for Daniel, and for Galia. You're not going to write terrible things about me, I think.

Amos's self-confrontation at this penultimate moment is unblinking. He can say these scathing things about himself because, after all, he trusts Nurith as a friend; he can admit to her that there has been something deeply hidden and perhaps even inauthentic about him as a person. What could he have meant? Much of this, I will suggest, goes back to his childhood and those doting but problematic parents who imprinted on him the role of performer. It is a role for which he had a natural gift, but he sensed that it was, in his own phrase, a masquerade. He could charm, he could entertain, he could seduce, and exerting that skill had an intoxicating effect on him. It rarely played any part in his writing. Here I recall words from the great consecration scene in *A Tale of Love and Darkness*, in which he heard "a voice that brooks neither laughter nor frivolity." The phrase is borrowed from a moment of pitiless truth at the very end of Agnon's *Only Yesterday*. In the best of Amos's fiction, he plumbed the depths of his own inner darkness, expressed his most intimate fears and doubts, his uncompromising perception of people and institutions, trying to please nobody. I wrote earlier about the gap between Amos's outward self-presentation and a subterranean self. If the outwardly visible person constantly sought, as he confesses to Nurith Gertz, to be liked and admired, the subterranean self was not merely plagued by demons but felt that he was not worthy of admiration. What played a crucial role in this feeling, as in so much else, was his mother's suicide. Even though he had summoned the courage to imagine that terrible act as a writer, it continued to haunt him till the very end. He talks about it to Nurith at some length:

Write it, tell that ever since this guy was a twelve-and-a-half-year-old child and his mom went away, through all the years deep inside him he felt that he was not worth anything, never mind how much the world spoiled him and into how many languages he was translated and how many articles they wrote about him and how many copies of his books were sold. The whole time he fought against the feeling that he was not worth anything; the whole time he was looking for someone to tell him, you are worth something, you are worth something. It's not actually a lack of love, it's a lack of a feeling of worth. Nothing can fill that pit. No success and no praise and no words. You are simply not worth anything as a person; as a man, too, you are not worth anything because the most important woman in the world for you got up and slammed the door on you and went away.

He continues in this vein, adding this devastating conclusion: "If I had been worth loving, it wouldn't have happened, and it couldn't have happened. No mom would do this to her kid unless she didn't love him."

Ultimately, Amos Oz, the engaging public person, proves to be a tragic figure. We may recall in this connection a famous essay Edmund Wilson wrote many decades ago, "The Wound and the Bow," in which he proposes that artists produce their powerful art from the anguish of festering inner wounds. In a late interview, Amos said much the same thing. I do not mean to suggest that Amos Oz would not have been the strong writer he was without his mother's suicide, but he would certainly have been a different kind of writer. The appropriate response to the man and his life is admiration for the writer and compassion for the man.

The split I have proposed between the subterranean self and the crafted public persona needs one modification. There was also an authentic private Amos Oz who was neither demon-ridden nor calculating to create an effect through a public persona. This was the person compellingly manifested in his most intimate relationships, with his family and with his closest friends. As his death approached, he came to feel that his private self was, after all, what was most important to him. Nurith Gertz reports: "At the end of 2018 he will list for me the good things that happened in his life and will not mention prizes or medals and not even books, only people. Human connections, the children, the grandchildren, nothing more." To Nurith, he adds a wry comment: "And Nily, after his death, will sum it up—57 awards, the grand sum." Elsewhere, in the remark I have quoted about how much his children meant to him, he names them: Fania, Daniel, Galia. He begins with his eldest, skips to the youngest, and puts Galia at the end. This is not, I think, because he means to devalue her but rather because, since she has been such a painful trial for him, he momentarily chokes up, hesitating before he mentions her. It is precisely the care he felt for her that made her total rejection of him in his last seven years such a sharp torment. The ultimate test of a person's humanity is in his capacity to love, and whatever the calculations and theatricality in his negotiations with the public, he had that capacity in abundance. Of Nily, he says to Nurith Gertz, "I have loved that girl since I was a fifteen-year-old kid. I have loved her my whole life."

With Nurith Gertz he shares a complicated reflection about the role of love for him. He prefaces it by expressing a thought that underlies both his politics and his general sense of life: "I never bought the story of redemption, I never believed in it even for a moment. Not in the great renewal and not in this redemption. I believed that things would be better, that everything would be better, but I did not believe in this sweet redemption, I never believed in it." From redemption he moves on to love, perhaps because of the persistent general notion that love will redeem us: "I looked for love. I wanted people to love me. I wanted to love and for people to love me, and I had no one to love and no one loved me. It's much simpler than redemption." He is definitely not talking here about his relationship with Nily—he said he loved her all his life, and he had no reason to doubt that she returned that love. He is speaking here of a virtually cosmic love, one in which, as he goes on to say, everything will love him—the animals, the distant hills, the woods—and he will love everything. As his good friend Nurith remarks, this sounds a lot like redemption. Perhaps this is in part what he hoped to attain through his books. (Yehuda Amichai once said to me that he wrote so that people would love him.) Perhaps the extravagance of this fantasy of love is a compensation for the loss of his mother's love because, as we have seen, he felt she brutally tore herself away from him forever. Nevertheless, he was content enough in his loving intimacy with Nily, with Fania, with Daniel, with his grandchildren, and he longed to have that with Galia as well, though she denied it to him.

An additional aspect of the private person who neither was pursued by darkness nor basked in the limelight was humor. In one of his talks, Amos remarked that he was never much of a source of humor, in contrast to his son, Daniel. He confesses to Shira Hadad that there is no sign of humor in his earlier writing and perhaps not anywhere. There are humorous moments in his public presentations, though these might be seen as part of his effort to beguile his audience. But *A Tale of Love and Darkness* incorporates scenes of vivid comedy, demonstrating in its overall configuration as a book that humor can coexist with anguish and bleakness. David Grossman remarked after Amos's death that he keenly missed him, missed especially the telephone conversations filled with humor: "In general we think of Amos Oz as a sober, grave, serious person. He also knew how to make you laugh and to laugh about himself." This aspect of Amos is worth mentioning because humor in personal relationships has to be spontaneous; it cannot be faked. Its expression by Amos is evidence of a man not always wracked by suppressed anguish and self-doubt and not always projecting a persona but also someone thoroughly engaging to his intimates.

Shira Hadad's late conversations with Amos devote more space than those of Nurith Gertz to his feelings about his writing, perhaps because their friendship came about through her role as his editor, though she does include that revealing set of exchanges on his views about women and sex. He tells her about his relentless dedication to revision, which he had talked about elsewhere, though here he reveals that he worked on one novel for a year and then, still dissatisfied, discarded it. He admits that he came to view the highly wrought language of *Where the Jackals Howl* as a mistake. He was in his early twenties when he wrote those stories, and he confesses that the style reflected a lack of confidence, a self-conscious assertion of: Look at me, I can write this really fancy Hebrew! He prudently remarks, "When I began writing, I was tight-assed. I thought there were things simply beneath the dignity of literature."

Shira Hadad pushes him to say how he felt about negative criticism as his career went on. She is referring to Israeli critics, who became, she proposes, more severe toward him after the publication of *Touch the Water, Touch the Wind* in 1973, and perhaps still more nine years later, with the appearance of *A Perfect Peace. Touch the Water, Touch the Wind* is in fact flawed in ways that make it vulnerable to criticism; *A Perfect Peace*, in my view, is a relatively strong novel. Some of the negative response confirms the adage that no man is a prophet in his own country. Amos tells Shira that he has no explanation for this shift in critical opinion but that he was hurt by the more vehement attacks. Even the enthusiasm for his early work was by no means unanimous, however, and there were emphatic denigrators from the beginning. At another point in these conversations Amos says that he paid attention to the criticism of the high style in

Where the Jackals Howl, which helped him to realize that he needed to turn down the volume.

Amos had had no inclination to reread his books, he remarks to Shira Hadad, viewing them as ancient history with no relevance to where he had come afterward as a writer. Interestingly, he makes a single exception for *The Same Sea,* to which he finds himself going back repeatedly. It is so different, he says, from everything else he has written, "that I simply can't believe that I wrote it. Altogether, I don't relate to it as my book. Don't know where it came from. It passed through me and came out on the other side." I would connect his sense of *The Same Sea* as a kind of spontaneous eruption, or perhaps, a virgin birth, with its lyric form, through which the book taps into autobiographical depths, both directly and obliquely, in a way that none of his other novels do.

Amos's conversation with Shira Hadad on the critics of his fiction takes a somewhat surprising turn when, without transition, he jumps from literature to politics. Speaking about himself in the third person, which amuses his interlocutor, he says "that he didn't exactly get along, not with the post-Zionist Left, not with the defeatists who have given up on Israel, not with the sentimental nationalists who claim Israel is a light unto the nations, nor with those who say the Arabs are not guilty of anything or those who say they are guilty of everything." The reasons that would produce objections to his writing and objections to his politics are altogether different in kind, of course. He speaks of them in one breath, I think, because in the two roles in which he presented himself to the Israeli public, the novelist and the political activist, he was forced to see that he could never please everybody; at times he felt he could please nobody. He was not haunted by this awareness but accepted it with a certain resignation; it also at times made life trying.

The last of the conversations with Shira Hadad—at any

rate, as she has chosen to place it—goes through several topics previously dealt with: his writing, his political activism, his views on the conflict with the Palestinians. In the concluding pages, however, the flow of the conversation brings Amos to say several things that illuminate his sense of his life at a moment when he realized it would soon be over. Shira Hadad remarks that she has never detected expressions of despair in his writing. In discussing his political stance, I, too, remarked that it was characterized by a stubborn optimism. Here he says something a little different:

> I don't despair because I know that living is like driving a car in which the windshield is completely covered, and you have only the side mirrors in which you can see what's behind. We know what was, not what waits ahead. Don't get me wrong, it's not that I'm an eternal optimist. About some things I'm a pessimist. But my pessimism is sweetened by the fact that I love people and I'm attached to them. I don't have a shred of misanthropy.

The metaphor he chooses suggests a sense of life in which the future not only is unknown but could be scarily dangerous. That notion may make sense for someone who lived for almost eighty years in one of the world's most dangerous neighborhoods. But the swing to the "sweetening" of pessimism is telling. Amos Oz, the orphaned soul, isolated in his often bleak childhood, then an unhappy loner in his adolescence on the kibbutz, bears witness here that the love he has felt for people—for Nily, for his children and grandchildren, for his intimate friends—has given him a certain faith in life. This is a kind of triumph for a person who started out in what he would represent metaphorically as a prison of a home and then was broken by a trauma that made him feel hopelessly abandoned in the world.

Near the end of these final conversations, Shira Hadad asks Amos if he is concerned about aging, about death. This is hardly an abstract question to pose to a man with terminal cancer. The first part of his response manifests that concentration of mind before an imminent execution of which Dr. Johnson spoke:

> Why, after all, are we so afraid of death? Some a bit more, some a bit less, but all of us are afraid of it. Look, the world existed billions of years before we were born, without us, and it will exist billions of years after we are no longer here. We are a kind of flickering, a transient flash. If that's the case, tell me, why should the black abyss after death especially frighten us?

To this he adds, "I was already in the black abyss of absolute extinction before I was born. Millions of years I was there, and it wasn't that bad for me. Why should it be so bad to be there again?" These reflections are rather like the haunting first sentence of Nabokov's great autobiography, *Speak, Memory:* "The cradle rocks above the abyss, and common sense tells us that our existence is but a brief crack of light between two eternities of darkness." Nabokov goes on in the body of the book to show how warmly luminous that brief crack of light can be, and I think the same is true for Amos's sense of life.

As Amos continues with this meditation on death, he invokes—misquoting the last word—the verse from Job that he had introduced into the thoughts of Riko in *The Same Sea,* twenty years earlier: "Naked I came out from my mother's womb and naked shall I return there." From this verse, he develops a little schema of human life: "The verse . . . promises us that after death we return exactly to the place we came out of: our mother's womb. And after all, the place we came out of was not bad: to come out of the womb, to make some noise, to run around, buy things, travel, come back, love, make an impression, to get excited, disappointed, and then simply return to the womb? Okay, why not? After all, there, in the womb, we are looked after, nurtured, enveloped in warmth and softness, and there are no worries there." This reflection on the line of poetry from Job is the consoling fantasy of the person who had irrevocably lost his mother at the age of twelve: death is now imagined as a restoration of that terrible loss, a return to the original maternal haven.

But he cannot permit himself to rest in this consolation. When Shira Hadad asks him then if he is unafraid of death, he answers frankly, "What I've said to you is what I say to myself while I tremble in great fear of death." The verse from Job provides him, he explains, momentary comfort, but it does not altogether drive away the fear. He adds: "I'm not prepared to die this evening or tomorrow morning, happy and cheerful. Definitely not. Because finally I find it very interesting here. Even the terrible and ghastly things are interesting." This is very much the voice of Amos Oz the novelist, the writer who held up curiosity as a cardinal virtue, who wrote because he was fascinated by the dizzying range of human types and behaviors and by how social institutions, ideologies, politics, and history shaped people and their actions. We all come, sooner or later, to our ineluctable end, but it attests to a kind of resilience of spirit that Amos, even as he was shaken by fear of the end closing in on him, did not abandon his novelist's curiosity that had impelled him to follow so many of the unpredictable combinations and permutations of the human condition.

Most of us bear within us certain stubborn contradictions of character, and this was abundantly evident in Amos Oz. (In fact, we should perhaps be wary of a person who is completely consistent in all things.) Amos was plagued with doubts about his self-worth, haunted by the trauma in his childhood, repeatedly drawn in his fiction to ponder the dark, self-destructive side of human nature, and often unable to shake loose from his role as a public performer, that constant masquerade he spoke of to Nurith Gertz. And yet he embraced the world around him with an eagerness of fascination; he was able to love his wife, his children, his grandchildren, and his dearest friends, both men and women, unreservedly; he could be spontaneous and funny;

and for all his delving as a writer into the murky depths of people, he was staunchly committed to the importance of reason in human affairs, especially in the realm of politics.

The course of his career as a novelist manifested a particularly strong contradiction. Everything he wrote was rooted in the reality of Israel—its history from before the establishment of the State, its culture, its clash of ideologies, the variety of human types it encompassed. Occasionally I wonder what someone reading him in translation can make of his through-and-through Israeli characters and their unfamiliar cultural contexts. What, for example, can a reader in New York or Milan or Berlin fathom of a character such as Shraga Ungar, the grandiose, paranoid, obsessive protagonist of the novella *Late Love*, for decades a lecturer on the kibbutz circuit, fixated on the evils of the Soviet Union, from which he fled, and equally on the figure of Moshe Dayan, to whom he looks to save his mortally endangered nation? Yet the novels and stories of Amos Oz have exerted a powerful magnetism for countless readers far removed from the thoroughly Israeli settings of the plots. Their appeal was generated by his gifts as a writer, but it may also have something to do with the extremeness and vehemence of Israel's human types and of the historical and political challenges with which they struggle, the fact that Israel is a kind of laboratory for the study of the possibilities of character and behavior. All this seems to have proved deeply interesting to readers who have barely thought about Zionism, are not much engaged in the ongoing conflict between Arab and Jew, and have no reason to care about the social and political reality of Mandatory Jerusalem or of Israel's kibbutzim and cooperative villages.

The concluding sentences of *Dear Zealot*, published two years before Amos's death, convey the roiling strangeness of the Israeli world, as well as his own unabated enthusiasm for contemplating that world. Ultimately, these valedictory words show how fascinated he remained by all he observed around him. It was this fascination that made him a novelist, that imparted a buoyancy to his life, despite the personal demons with which he wrestled.

It's good for me to be the citizen of a state in which there are eight and a half million prime ministers, eight and a half million prophets, eight and a half million messiahs. Each of us with his personal version of redemption or at least of a solution. All of them shout, only a few listen. It's not boring here. It is of course provoking, infuriating, disappointing, sometimes even triggering frustration and fury, but also quite often riveting and stirring. What I've seen here in my lifetime is a lot less and also a lot more than my parents and the parents of my parents ever dreamed.

------◆|◆|◆------

Epilogue

READERS OF THIS BOOK will have realized from the first chapter that it is not the kind of biography that chronicles the comings and goings and doings of its subject month by month. That approach often generates tomes of a thousand pages that may provide a useful factual archive of a life. The portrait, however, of the distinctive living person in such presentations often remains a little faint. What I have sought to do reflects an opposite approach to biography. Amos Oz was a complicated man. In certain ways, he was not altogether the person he was generally perceived to be. The obvious reason that we should at all be interested in his life is that he created a body of work that has powerfully engaged a broad readership, first in his own country and in due course across the world. There are lapses among his many books; late in life he himself conceded that at least two of his novels fell short. Yet he achieved what few writers do, fashioning through his painstaking writing process several works of fiction that will endure.

In a few instances the novels and stories directly reflect the circumstances of his life, although more often the reflection is oblique or significantly transformed. In any case, to "decode" his fiction as a representation of his life would be a mistake, as it would be, conversely, to imagine that his life explains his fiction. What I have undertaken is to bring various direct testimonies— by him and by those close enough to him to know about his fears, his aspirations, his self-doubts, what was important to him, and what he had undergone—together with readings of a few of his central books that appear to draw on the inner world of the man. The best of his books are compelling as imaginative takes on a range of human types and on the social and political realm to which he belonged. In discussing his life I have tried to honor his fiction as a series of imaginative creations that do not necessarily manifest his own experience.

As a friend of Amos, I had certain views on the kind of person he was. But the documentation of his life that I looked into in undertaking the biography made me aware that there were dimensions of his character I could not have seen. Perhaps the essential understanding I came to is that his was a life courageously lived. To the very end he was plagued by dark, devastating thoughts he could never shake. What he possessed to confront them was his strong talent—not only as a writer but as a public advocate for his views on literature and on his nation's vexed political and social dilemmas. Despite the burden of bleakness he carried with him from childhood till his last days, he never slid into depression, never succumbed to the temptation of escape through intoxicants. Instead, he was actuated by a sense that he had tasks to perform in this world. He relished writing and reveled in deploying the rich resources of the Hebrew language that was his medium. At the same time, as the words he chose for the crucial dedication scene in *A Tale of Love and Dark-ness* strongly suggest, he felt that for him to take in the world by writing about it was a demanding moral obligation, one that "brooks neither frivolity nor laughter." He met that obligation, often with impressive success, throughout his life. In a very different way, he felt an obligation to use his talents as a responsible citizen to address his nation's besetting political problems and the fraught moral consequences they entailed. I suspect that conscientiously fulfilling this double demand helped him to push back his private demons, keeping them from leading him to any self-subverting effects they might have entailed.

Duty to the writer's vocation and duty to addressing the fate of the nation did not exhaust the life he bravely lived. There were also impulses of spontaneity—in his gift for friendship, in his moments of humor, and, above all, in his capacity for love. At the age of twelve and a half, the person he loved most abandoned him (again and again, he would see his mother's suicide as a brutal abandonment of her young son). For the next sixty-seven years, he repeatedly interpreted this as her way of saying that she had never really loved him. But where did that harsh conclusion leave him in regard to love in his own life? There are blighted souls who are incapable of love, but Amos was not one of them. He loved Nily, who was initially linked with him in an adolescent friendship that turned into a *coup de foudre* for both of them at the age of twenty and that lasted a lifetime. He loved all three of his children, despite the torment that came to cloud his relationship with one of them during his last seven years. And he genuinely loved his closest friends, men and women.

Was he a happy man? The available evidence may indicate that he was, though perhaps only intermittently. What is moving about the life of Amos Oz is that it was finally a kind of triumph against heavy odds. The triumph lies not just in the literary achievement of his finest work but in the identity he managed to sustain as a loving husband, father, and friend, as a dedicated writer exploring the limits of his art, and as an Israeli citizen driven by an imperative of conscience. His was not an easy life, but finally it was a fulfilled life, not only artistically but morally.

INDEX

Amos Oz is referred to as "Amos" in index sublevel entries. His writings are listed by title or at "Oz, Amos, writings by."

at kibbutz, 35–36, 149; at Monash University (Melbourne), 105; named for Amos's mother, 45; Oxford studies of, 92; relationship with her father, 95–98, 105, 154–55, 165

Oz, Galia (daughter): Amos speaking about, at end of his life, 95, 154; in car crash when Amos was driving (1976), 52; as children's author, 78; estrangement from her father, 95–99, 113, 154, 155, 165; at kibbutz, 35–36, 149; *Something That Pretends to Be Love*, 96

Oz, Nily Zuckerman (wife): on Amos as orphan, 35, 43, 75; Amos's love for, 154–55, 165; Amos's marriage proposal to, 45; on Amos's political involvement, 14; Amos's tributes to, 93, 95; Amos telling her of his mother's suicide, 4, 5, 67; in Arad, 78; army service of, 44; in car crash when Amos was driving (1976), 52; dancing and *joie de vivre* of, 44–45; dislike of Amos's smoking, 37; on Galia-Amos relationship, 96; her father, 42; international travel with Amos, 71, 99; life at kibbutz as wife and mother, 149; marriage, 45–46, 93, 97; meeting Amos at kibbutz, 35, 42–43; on military directives written by Amos, 49; personality of, 43; reminiscences of Amos after his death, 98

Palestinians: in agreement with Amos's views, 119; the dream of the pre-1948 landscape, 133–34; journal editor in East Jerusalem, 117, 119; the need to recognize Israeli right to a state, 133; the idea of the one-state solution ending up with Palestinian control, 127; portrayal as the Other, 70; treatment of, 90. *See also* Gaza Strip; Israeli-Palestinian conflict; *A Journey in the Land of Israel*; Occupied Territories; West Bank

Palmach, 48

Peace Now movement, 52

Peretz, Y. L., 17

Picasso, Pablo: *The Tragedy*, 7

politics: Amos as pluralist, 118, 120–22, 125–26, 130–31; Amos as socialist, 27, 31, 149; Amos in Peace Now movement, 52; Amos's opinions sought by Israeli politicians, 39; Amos's opposition to fanaticism, 25, 64–65, 73, 80–81, 86, 127, 130–31, 150; Left vs. Right split, 24–25, 121; liberal, 121, 130; peaceful reconciliation with Palestinians, 70, 85; Zionism and party affiliations, 24–25. *See also* activist, Amos as

Prohibition Era, Jewish gangsters in, 112

prophets (biblical), 50, 81, 112

public speaker, Amos as, 100–111; analogy, use of, 102–3; charisma and engagement with groups, 29, 72, 89–90, 101, 104–5, 111, 113, 152; childhood roots of performing, 95, 100, 152; in English, 59, 100–101, 105; in English compared to Hebrew, 104–5; on fiction writing, 103–4; in Hebrew, 101–2; international travel for speaking engagements, 98–99, 109; on Israel and Israeli-Palestinian conflict, 105, 107–8, 115; on Jews as group who doubt and argue, 106–7; oversimplification of, 106–7; performance mode, 89, 94–95; time and energy expended, 109, 115, 131; writing not affected by, 109–11. *See also* activist, Amos as; *specific talks by location*

Rabin, Yitzhak, 85

Rehavia (Jerusalem high school), 31

Revisionist Zionists, 24

Jewish Lives is a prizewinning series of interpretative biography designed to explore the many facets of Jewish identity. Individual volumes illuminate the imprint of Jewish figures upon literature, religion, philosophy, politics, cultural and economic life, and the arts and sciences. Subjects are paired with authors to elicit lively, deeply informed books that explore the range and depth of the Jewish experience from antiquity to the present.

Jewish Lives is a partnership of Yale University Press and the Leon D. Black Foundation. Ileene Smith is editorial director. Anita Shapira and Steven J. Zipperstein are series editors.

Mark Rothko: Toward the Light in the Chapel, by Annie Cohen-Solal
Ruth: A Migrant's Tale, by Ilana Pardes
Gershom Scholem: Master of the Kabbalah, by David Biale
Bugsy Siegel: The Dark Side of the American Dream,
 by Michael Shnayerson
Solomon: The Lure of Wisdom, by Steven Weitzman
Steven Spielberg: A Life in Films, by Molly Haskell
Alfred Stieglitz: Taking Pictures, Making Painters, by Phyllis Rose
Barbra Streisand: Redefining Beauty, Femininity, and Power,
 by Neal Gabler
Leon Trotsky: A Revolutionary's Life, by Joshua Rubenstein
Warner Bros: The Making of an American Movie Studio,
 by David Thomson
Elie Wiesel: Confronting the Silence, by Joseph Berger

FORTHCOMING TITLES INCLUDE:

Abraham, by Anthony Julius
Hannah Arendt, by Masha Gessen
Walter Benjamin, by Peter Gordon
Franz Boas, by Noga Arikha
Alfred Dreyfus, by Maurice Samuels
Anne Frank, by Ruth Franklin
George Gershwin, by Gary Giddins
Herod, by Martin Goodman
Jesus, by Jack Miles
Josephus, by Daniel Boyarin
Louis Kahn, by Gini Alhadeff
Mordecai Kaplan, by Jenna Weissman Joselit
Carole King, by Jane Eisner
Fiorello La Guardia, by Brenda Wineapple
Hedy Lamarr, by Sarah Wildman